James Edward McGee

The men of '48

Being a brief history of the repeal association and the Irish confederation

James Edward McGee

The men of '48
Being a brief history of the repeal association and the Irish confederation

ISBN/EAN: 9783337124939

Printed in Europe, USA, Canada, Australia, Japan

Cover: Foto ©ninafisch / pixelio.de

More available books at **www.hansebooks.com**

THE MEN OF '48.

BEING A BRIEF HISTORY OF THE REPEAL ASSOCIATION AND THE IRISH CONFEDERATION; WITH BIOGRAPHICAL SKETCHES OF THE LEADING ACTORS IN THE LATTER ORGANIZATION, THEIR PRINCIPLES, OPINIONS, AND LITERARY LABORS.

BY

COL. JAMES E. McGEE,

AUTHOR OF "IRISH SOLDIERS IN EVERY LAND," "LIVES OF IRISHMEN'S SONS," ETC.

IN ONE VOLUME.

BOSTON:
D. O'LOUGHLIN,
IRISH NATIONAL PUBLISHING HOUSE,
630 Washington Street.

CONTENTS.

CHAPTER I.

PAGE.

Introductory—Ireland's second greatest grievance—The Act of Union—Debasement of the Irish people—Daniel O'Connell—Catholic struggles for civil rights—The Emancipation Act of 1829—Agrarian agitation—Symptoms of a Repeal movement. - - - - - - - 9

CHAPTER II.

The Repeal Association—Establishment of the *Nation*—Thomas Davis—His birth and education—Views on National subjects—Prose and Poetry—Influence on Irish literature—Death—Opinions of his cotemporaries. - - - 29

CHAPTER III.

The Repeal year—Monster Meetings—The *Nation*—Opening of Conciliation Hall—William Smith O'Brien—His birth and descent—Career in parliament—Joins the Repeal Association. - 48

CHAPTER IV.

Arrest of O'Connell, John O'Connell, Duffy, Gray, Barrett, Ray, Steele, Rev. Fathers Tyrrell and Tierney—Feeling of the country—State Trials—Conviction—Effect in Parliament—Sentence and Imprisonment—More troops for Ireland—Reversal of Judgment—General rejoicing. - 76

CONTENTS.

CHAPTER V.

State of the Country—Its prosperity, resources, and revenue—Diminution of Crime—Rev. Theobald Mathew—His birth, education, and services—His political views—Effect of his labors in the National cause—Affection for the "Young Irelanders"—O'Connell's and O'Brien's eulogies on his character. - - - - - - - - - 93

CHAPTER VI.

Symptoms of disunion in the Repeal Association—Charitable Bequests bill—Federalism advocated by O'Connell—Denounced by the *Nation* and O'Neil Daunt—English intrigues at Rome—The Papal Rescript—Financial reforms proposed—Formation of the '82 Club—The Queen's Colleges bill—The Irish Hierarchy on education. - 112

CHAPTER VII.

Celebration of the first anniversary of the 30th of May, 1844—O'Connell in Thurles—Action of the British parliament respecting absent members—Michael Doheny—William Smith O'Brien and John O'Connell—Imprisonment of the former, dereliction of the latter—Debate in Conciliation Hall—Address of the '82 Club—More dissensions—Approach of the Famine. - - - 140

CHAPTER VIII.

Opening of Parliament—Coercion and Free Trade—O'Connell and O'Brien in London—Defeat of the Tories—The Whigs in office—Conciliation Hall defies them—Thomas Francis Meagher—Repeal abandoned—O'Gorman, Mitchel, and Doheny—

O'Connell's strange course—Trial of Charles Gavan Duffy—Peace Resolutions—Secession from the Association. - - - - - 166

CHAPTER IX.

O'Brien's account of the secession—Attempts at a reconciliation—The "Old Irelanders" in favor of place-taking—The Dublin Remonstrants—Thomas D'Arcy McGee—Position of the *Nation*—Whig treachery—O'Connell in Parliament—Progress of the Famine. - - - - - 197

CHAPTER X.

Attempts at reunion—John B. Dillon—The Irish Confederation—Its organization and aims—The Galway election—More overtures for union—Charles Gavan Duffy—Rev. C. P. Meehan. - 218

CHAPTER XI.

The American-Irish Banquet—Richard O'Gorman, Jr.—A truce proposed—O'Brien in the Confederation—A disgraceful scene in Conciliation Hall—Rev. Mr. McHugh—Death of O'Connell—Its effects on the people—Fate of Conciliation Hall—The *Nation* on the future—Election in Cork, a Confederate victory. - - - - - 242

CHAPTER XII.

The General Election of 1847—J. O'Connell withdraws from Dublin—O'Brien reëlected for Limerick—Meagher in Waterford—The Repeal members—Grattan on the Famine—The Irish Council—The Confederate clubs—Division in the Confederation—John Mitchel—meeting in Dublin—The French Revolution of 1848—Its effects on Ireland—Deputation to Paris—Arrests—Transportation of Mitchel—End of the old *Nation*. - - - - - - - 260

CHAPTER XIII.

Attempts at insurrection in the south—The affair of Ballingarry—Escape of Dillon, Doheny, O'Gorman, and McGee—Arrest of O'Brien, Meagher, O'Donohoe, and McManus—their trial and conviction—O'Brien's intrepidity—Character of O'Donohoe and McManus—Meagher's speech—Last of the Irish Confederation. - - - 286

CHAPTER XIV.

The literature of the "Young Ireland" party—James Clarence Mangan—Denis Florence McCarthy—Richard D'Alton Williams Lady Wilde—The Library of Ireland—Davis, Duffy, Father Meehan, Doheny, McNevin, Mitchel, McGee, McCarthy, and Mrs. Callan—Their legacy to "Young Ireland" of to day. - - - 299

PREFACE.

RECENT advices from Europe indicate that the struggle for self-government and the right of domestic legislation, which has been suspended in Ireland since 1848, is about to be renewed; and, it is to be hoped, under more favorable auspices than those which ushered in the Repeal movement under O'Connell, or the Irish Confederation of Duffy and O'Brien. Men, almost entirely new to the mass of the people, seem to be taking the most prominent part in this revived agitation; and a generation, who know little of the virtues and faults, the victories and defeats, which characterized the popular leaders of 1840-50, are their followers.

As, in conducting this new crusade against English misgovernment, those champions of national rights will have to go over much of the ground trodden by their predecessors, they will, if they hope for success, be obliged to avoid and overcome the pitfalls and obstacles which entrapped or retarded the men of '43 and '48 in their progress towards independence. "Sweet are the uses of adversity;" and from the misfortunes of the past may be gleaned many valuable lessons for the guidance of the present generation.

It was partially with this purpose in view that I have written this volume; for, though it may not find many readers on the other side of the Atlantic, it will not be without its influence here. America and Ireland are now so intimately connected by ties of blood, mutual interest, and a common appreciation of the advantages of free government, that nothing which concerns the one can be without interest to the other. In these days of the rapid transmission of intelligence, public opinion, in either hemisphere, is constantly acting and reacting upon the people and government of both.

But what I designed principally was to present to those of my countrymen in the United States, who personally remember something of the Repeal Agitation under the great O'Connell and the Irish Confederates, a brief and, as far as possible, an accurate account of the origin, growth, and culmination of the differences which, in the year 1846, grew up in the Repeal Association; as well as to convey some true ideas of the character, opinions, aims, and mental status of the sincere and gifted men who felt called upon to separate from the bulk of the Liberator's followers. In endeavoring to do so, I can safely say that I have not been actuated by any want of admiration for the genius or patriotism of that illustrious Irishman; nor influenced by any personal predilection for those who differed from him on what is now generally conceded, the high grounds of political faith and public duty.

As to the prominent members of the Irish Confederation, I am but too well aware that, smarting from recent defeat, and perhaps laboring under false impressions, they have said words of each other that had better not have been uttered, and which they themselves have regretted more deeply than any person: I have therefore striven to avoid, as much as possible, instituting invidious comparisons between men who were equal in honesty, in truthfulness, in devotion, and who only differed in mental attributes in degree.

If I have spoken harshly or slightingly in these pages of the attempts of the Confederates to produce an armed revolution in Ireland, it is because I would warn all others from the imitation of such a dangerous experiment in a country where the use of arms is unknown to the vast majority of the population, and where the only military knowledge possessed by Irishmen is unfortunately used in the enslavement of their country. The right of Ireland to secure complete independence, even by the utmost exertion of force, is, in my mind, unquestionable; but no people, no matter how badly governed, have a right to adopt this ultimate alternative without the moral probability of success. Nor, indeed, is any man, no matter how distinguished or experienced, justified in exciting his fellow-beings to arms, who is not prepared to show that he has the capacity to lead them, and reasonable means to insure their success.

For many of the facts and incidents related in this volume, I have been indebted to the cotemporary files of the *Nation* and Dublin *Freeman*, to Mitchel's "Last Conquest of Ireland—Perhaps;" Doheny's "Felon's Track;" the letters and personal statements of many of the chief actors in the scenes related; and to several volumes of the *N. Y. Truth-Teller*, kindly furnished me by the late Mr. William McN. Denman.

J. E. M.

New York:—St. Patrick's Day, 1874.

CHAPTER I.

Introductory—Ireland's second greatest grievance—The Act of Union—Debasement of the Irish people—Daniel O'Connell—Catholic struggles for civil rights—The Emancipation act of 1829—Agrarian agitation—Symptoms of a Repeal movement.

THE greatest misfortune that has ever befallen the people of Ireland, always excepting the loss of her national independence, was the deprivation of her legislative power, and consequently of the right of her people to make their own laws, subject only to the supervision of the monarch of the United Kingdoms.

The first calamity was brought about by slow degrees, as well as by an almost endless series of desultory battles, wholesale confiscations, and unparalleled atrocities. If we examine the records of Anglo-Norman conquest in Ireland, from the invasion in 1169 down to the "pacification" of Mountjoy in the time of Elizabeth, we will find that it required more than four hundred years of continual warfare, undertaken by a power far more numerous and wealthy, and assisted by mercenaries from the Continent, to overwhelm, for the time at least, that perennial spring of patriotism and bravery which flows so purely and strongly from the Gaelic heart.

Other countries, notably England herself, have been conquered in a couple of campaigns or even in a single battle. The Romans found little difficulty in subduing the primitive barbarians of Albion; Hengist and Horsa literally swept the Britons off the face of the soil and drove them into the recesses of the Welsh mountains, from which they never returned; and the descendants of those very Saxons, in the eleventh century, were in turn trampled upon and enslaved by William's *filibusteros*, without let or hinderance, after his first battle, Hastings. A century latter saw the descendants of those very conquerors in Ireland, equally as ready for spoliation and confiscation; but their success was not commensurate with their hopes or advantages. William's

"Normans" were gathered from the four winds of heaven, and from all classes of society: men of desperate fortunes, and with consciences not over-scrupulous, though brave and experienced soldiers. Those of their progeny who went to Ireland were very much of the same caste and character; for as yet the baser Saxon blood had not been allowed to commingle with the supposed purer strain of their masters. They had this advantage, also, over their ancestors: that, as the military art was becoming more and more developed on the Continent, the interminable wars of the earlier Norman kings, in defence of their territorial rights in France, gave them ample opportunities of becoming skilled and intrepid warriors: an advantage totally beyond the reach of an insular and isolated people like the Irish of that period.

In building, defending, and assailing fortifications, they had no superiors in Europe; and, though their strategy was primitive and their tactics simple, they were vastly in advance of the Irish in their mode of initiating and conducting a campaign, as well as in the excellence of their armor and weapons of war—in everything, in fact, that leads to successful warfare, except courage and an unyielding spirit of resistance.

Yet with all those advantages on their side, the Anglo-Normans made little progress in their conquests for the first two or three centuries after their arrival, and it may be safely asserted that there was no time between the reign of the second and that of the eighth Henry—a period of nearly four centuries—that the Irish princes and chiefs, if united, might not easily have driven their invaders from the country as the Northmen had been expelled by their forefathers, when

> "Malachy conquered the foeman, and Brian uprooted the Dane."

But sectional jealousy and personal spite were always in the ascendant in the councils of the Irish chiefs, even while the star of their country's independence was setting red in the blood of her chivalrous sons. Then came the quasi Irish parliaments of the Pale, who very generously voted—what did not belong to them to give—the crown of Ireland to that monster of iniquity Henry VIII. For this gracious act of munificence, as well as for turning over body and soul from the ancient faith to the new reformation, the pliant tools were liberally rewarded by their august master with grants of abbey and church lands, and the revenues of pillaged hospitals, colleges, and nunneries. It is unnecessary to say that the terms of the bargain were mutually satisfactory.

Henceforward the so-called Irish parliament was always to be found the most obedient, humble servant of the English officials; and nothing was so sycophantic or grovelling that it would not do, did its masters but intimate the slightest wish to that effect. It was of course a representative body only in name, for its benches were filled with placemen and pensioners; neither the people, nor even a fraction of the people, ever being consulted in its formation or advised of its doings. But it answered the purpose of its founders well enough, and became in course of time one of those agreeable delusions of the English system of government, by which the masses are led to believe that they are governed by a fixed constitution and equitable laws, made, in part at least, by their veritable representatives.

Toward the close of the last century, however, a change was becoming apparent in the tone and temper of the so-called national assembly. Every device and scheme that could be suggested to acute and intolerant minds had been used against the Catholic Irish until they were beggared, exiled, or driven to starvation; then their persecutors rested for a while in their headlong course, as it were, through sheer satiety. But there was still another code of laws which pressed heavily on the whole people, irrespective of creed or religion. A portion of the enactments under this sytem restricted the exportation of the produce of the soil to ports other than those of

England and a few of her colonies, while the markets of the world were virtually closed to her manufactures. As those laws had been passed by the English parliament, of course the Irish travesty upon it had no power to repeal or modify them. Now, as the landlords, directly or indirectly concerned in the exports of agricultural products, were invariably Protestants; and the manufacture and sale of linen, cloth, glass, etc., were almost exclusively monopolized by the Ulster Presbyterians, it followed that there was great dissatisfaction among that class of his Majesty's most faithful subjects. It was all very well to crush and humiliate the Catholics, then three-fourths of the population; but as soon as the lash was applied to the back of the dominant minority it was declared rank tyranny.

When the war of the American Revolution had drained Ireland of her usual defenders and jailers, the occasion was seized upon by this class to organize a national, unpaid militia, called the "Volunteers," who instead of at once taking possession of the government and declaring thorough independence of all foreign domination, which might have been done without the effusion of a drop of blood, boasted of their loyalty, of their readiness to fight against the French and Americans, declared the right of *Protestants* to bear arms, and demanded—unrestricted trade with foreign countries. This concession was quickly granted, as would any other that might have been required, simply because England had no power to refuse it. But there were some men, high-spirited, eloquent, and, to a certain extent, national in feeling, like Grattan, Flood, Charlemont, and Daly, who had ulterior motives, and who felt that the only security for the country (*i. e.*, the Protestant faction), was the complete independence of the parliament, and this also was conceded, after a brief show of opposition, in 1782. Then the Volunteers, flushed with victory, resolved to take a further step, and having secured the corporate independence of the legislature, determined to reform and purify it, by getting rid of the majority of its members, the paid creatures of the government or the representatives of rotten boroughs. They accordingly met in convention in Dublin in 1783, and having reiterated the sapient opinion that *Protestants* had a right to carry arms; that *Protestants* with a certain property qualification ought to be allowed to vote; and by inference none but " Protestants" had or ought to have either, they applied to parliament, through their representative, Harry Flood, a leading patriotic bigot, for a reform bill embodying their plans. But times had changed, the American war was over, and England had withdrawn her shattered forces from the New World once more to sustain her despotic power in the Old; while the mass of the Irish, the Catholics, who had so long encouraged and sustained the Volunteers, in hopes of obtaining some measure of justice through their aid, now, finding their confidence cruelly betrayed, and themselves declared unfit to bear a weapon for self-defence or to have the slightest share in making the laws, by the very men they had trusted so far, withdrew their assistance and the moral support of their overpowering numbers. Mr. Flood's bill was not only rejected by an immense majority, but he was not permitted even to introduce it in the accustomed form. From that time the Volunteers degenerated, and in a few years disappeared from the sight of men. The result of their labors, freedom of trade and legislative independence, vanished almost as quickly, if not so quietly.

England having thus effectually helped the Volunteers to destroy themselves, set to work systematically to annihilate the body which they had rendered independent, and by one bold stroke to abolish forever the assembly that had of late become so dangerous to her interests, commercially and politically. With one hand she petted and caressed the Catholics, and with the other she armed the Orangemen against them. She encouraged secret revolutionary societies while proclaiming martial law in the disturbed districts, and finally over the entire country. In turns she threatened the timid, bribed the venal, and allured, by false promises of speedy amelioration, the oppressed and persecuted. The object throughout was to win the good-will of the Catholics, who had no votes, but great physical power, while at the same time to secure a working majority of those who sat in parliament and of those whom they were supposed to represent. This line of policy was only partially successful, for it was found necessary to resort to more stringent measures before the popular voice would declare, or the slavish parliament vote for so execrable a measure as the destruction of their last shred of nationality. But Pitt, and his henchman, Castlereagh, were equal to the occasion. The unruly patient who would not consent to suicide must be treated to a little phlebotomy. Then commenced midnight murders by "Orangemen;" and retaliation by "Defenders;" quartering of brutal and licentious troops in the households of peaceful and virtuous families, half hanging, pitch-cap, triangle, and other like tortures, and, as if this were not enough to drive the most patient and most enduring people in the world to open rebellion, church burnings and wholesale massacres of the defenceless peasantry by the armed Orange yeomen were supplemented. Then followed, in rapid succession, the uprising of the gallant men of Wexford, the abortive attempts of the United Irishmen of the North, the arrest of the leaders of that organization in Dublin; trials by courts-martial, executions without number, and general terrorisms and stupefaction.

This was the opportune moment for the conspirators against the only remaining rights left to the nation. Bills to further cement the union of Ireland and England were simultaneously introduced into the parliaments of both countries, and in July, 1800, were passed by large majorities. To effect this unconstitutional and unexampled outrage on the liberties of the people, not only intimidation and cajolery were freely resorted to, but the most unblushing corruption and bribery were lavishly used; so repulsive was the deed even to those who most favored it secretly, or advocated its consummation with apparent candor.

From the first day of January, 1801, Ireland ceased to have even the semblance of nationality. Her laws in future were to be made in London, in a House of Commons seven-eighths of whose members had never seen Ireland or knew anything whatever of her resources, trade, commerce, or agriculture; and in a House of Lords where the ignorant majority was even more anti-Irish and anti-Catholic. Thus the country became, and so remains to this day, as much a portion of Great Britain, and as totally devoid of any political individuality, as Yorkshire or Kent, except when it subserves English designs to think otherwise; and then the comparative freedom of action and religious equality which is permitted those shires, are practically and unhesitatingly denied to one of the grandest and most illustrious of the old nations of Europe.

The condition of the Irish Catholics after the Union was humiliating and pitiful in the extreme. Weakened by the late civil struggle, betrayed by insidious advice into a partial support of the bill that took away the trifling rights yet remaining, and betrayed by those whom they had foolishly trusted, they found themselves without a leader or an advocate, scarcely daring to lift up their eyes to the Great Power above them, and ask His assistance to recover the opportunity they had so idly cast away. "In the public journals of the period," says a late writer, "they exhibit few symptoms of political life. They had lapsed into that drowsy torpor in which they are buried at present; and, as at present, the possibility of political action was precluded by the absence of political harmony. It was not consonant with the dignity of Catholics, as their aristocracy asserted, to address a parliament by which their petitions had been previously rejected. This insidious suggestion had the desired effect—it mummified the Catholic body. The same sophistry, under another form, has been employed in recent times to produce the same inaction. O'Connell dashed it aside. He was aware of the horror with which the titled sensualists who ruled the empire regarded agitation. To them, he knew that the irritation, the fret, which public meetings occasion is more annoying than violent and open war. Hence it was that O'Connell taught one uniform doctrine, Agitate! agitate! agitate!"

But even Daniel O'Connell, full of life, enthusiasm, energy, and eloquence as he then was, could not arouse the Catholic masses from their lethargy or instil into their degenerate souls one tittle of his own fire and manliness. In vain he organized Catholic Committees and Catholic Boards, in vain he denounced, with a wealth of language and a power of invective beyond conception, the illegality and utter injustice of the act of union and the diabolical atrocity of the penal laws; equally in vain did he try by example and precept to unite his oppressed co-religionists and infuse into their hearts some of his own hopefulness and moral courage. The terrors of '98 had entered into their very marrow, while the duplicity of those who sold their country for a mess of pottage sickened and disgusted them. A man with less pertinacity and determination than O'Connell would have given up the task in despair; as it was, he turned his attention more to his profession and to the preparation of those majestic forensic displays of wit, eloquence, and pathos—half legal, half political—which, while they seldom failed to convince the court and sway the jury, always served to electrify and arouse the plaudits of the audience. While he was waiting for a new generation he was schooling himself, and training the people for the great impending struggle for religious liberty which culminated in 1829.

This was inaugurated by O'Connell in the early part of 1823, by the formation of a Catholic Association, an organization which for more than a year after its inception attracted little attention and wielded no popular power. But when its objects and aims became gradually developed, the people and the priesthood flocked around its standards, till so dangerous had it become, in its numerical and moral strength, to English interests in Ireland, that an act was passed by the imperial parliament for its suppression. But the time had at length arrived when the new generation took the lead in public affairs without fear or hesitation. A few months after the dissolution of the first association another one was formed, and the people's demand for civil and religious rights was more thoroughly discussed and more persistently urged. The result was that George IV, acting under the direction of Wellington and the other members of his cabinet, signed the act of Emancipation on the 13th of April, 1829, and thus, as it was at the time said, placed the Catholics of Great Britain and Ireland on an equality with the Protestant sects.

The relief afforded the Catholics was not, however, either complete or unaccompanied by civil disabilities, some of which were removed by the Reform act, which opened the municipal corporations to Catholics; others in our own day by the Church Disestablishment bill, which abolished the tithe system; and many are still in existence. The old system of collecting tithes, it is true, was abandoned years ago; but being made a rent charge and payable by the owners of the land was no advantage to the tenants, as it was, of course, added to their already exorbitant rents. The reform bill of 1831 was an English measure, passed for the benefit of that people, and had very little influence for good or evil on Ireland. The disfranchisement of the forty shilling freeholders which had been made a condition of the passage of the Emancipation Act, was, under the circumstances then surrounding the peasant population, at best a negative evil.

The position of the Catholics was however substantially improved. O'Connell, in reward for his great services, was presented with the handsome sum of fifty thousand pounds sterling by his admiring co-religionists, and his presence everywhere throughout the country was hailed with the most enthusiastic demonstrations and tokens of gratitude by all classes.

But his late successes were but partial. He had obtained a great boon, it is true, for a portion of his country, and had destroyed a monster which had so long preyed on its vitals. Still he had only captured the outworks of the enemies' defences; the citadel remained in their possession. His former labors had been for the benefit of a class, he now intended to make them national. In other words, he proposed to unite all parties and creeds under one banner, with the common war-cry: Repeal of the Union. Too shrewd a man not to see that the cancer which was eating into the heart of Ireland could not be effectually cured by half measures introduced and mainly carried out by an alien parliament, and too proud a patriot to be content to see his native land in a state of worse than colonial dependence, he must have felt that, except the violent disruption of the Empire, there was no complete remedy for Irish grievances short of the restoration of her right of self-government. This was ever the burden of his speeches and addresses during the decade subsequent to emancipation, as well as through the whole course of his after life, while he had strength to raise his voice or wield his pen in behalf of his suffering countrymen.

From 1830 till 1840, there were spasmodic efforts made, from time to time, to enlist the sympathies of the entire people in favor of a repeal agitation, but with little or no effect. Some were satisfied with what they had obtained by the law of '29; others were more interested in local and agrarian matters; and still others, whose ambition rose no higher than keeping on terms with the English party in power for the sake of obtaining offices for themselves or friends, who attempted to use for selfish and degrading purposes the very provisions of the Emancipation Act, which allowed Catholics to hold office, not as an inducement for deserting the national cause, but as an absolute right and a token of religious equality.

CHAPTER II.

The Repeal Association—Establishment of the "Nation'—Thomas Davis—His birth and education—Views on national subjects—Prose and poetry—Influence on Irish literature—Death—Opinions of his contemporaries.

In 1840, the excitement that had attended the Reform, Tithe, and Municipal Reform bills had subsided. O'Connell and his colaborers, having had nearly ten years' experience in the imperial parliament, with ample opportunity to study the inclinations and views of the overwhelming majority of that body, found the sad conclusion forced on their minds that no hope for Ireland—no fair, impartial laws for her people—no adequate redress for her many grievances—could be expected from an assembly in which the wants of the country were neither recognized nor appreciated. Ignorance of Irish character and distress, and even of the very text and existence of the statutes of which most complaint had been made, was supplemented, in the case of the English,

Welsh, and Scotch members, by the most offensive display of superiority and condescension, which had at its root a bitter, hostile antipathy to the very name of Ireland.

O'Connell, therefore, disgusted but not disheartened, left his place in St. Stephen's and returned to Dublin, with a firm resolve to found an association for the purpose of restoring to the country her parliament; to arouse the dormant spirit of the nation to a sense of its degradation and of its strength; and to devote the few remaining years of his life—he was then sixty-four—to the consummation of his country's regeneration.

On the 15th of April, 1840, the first meeting of the new organization took place. It was held in the Corn Exchange building; about one hundred and fifty persons were present, the great Emancipator being the principal speaker on the occasion. In his opening address he said:

"My Fellow-Countrymen—I rise with the deep sense of the awful importance of the step I am about to propose to the Irish people, and a full knowledge of the difficulties by which we are surrounded and the obstacles we have to contend with. I trust that my heart is pure, and my judgment, on the present occasion, unclouded; and I declare in the presence of God, who is to judge me for an eternity of weal or woe, that I have no object in view but the good of my native land, and that I feel, in the deepest sense, the responsibility I am about to incur. We are about to enter on a struggle that will terminate only in having the most ample justice done to Ireland by placing her upon an equality with the sister-country, or in the establishment of our legislative independence. We commence under auspices that afford little prospect of ultimate success to some; but those who know the character of the brave, moral, religious, and patient Irish people, cannot be of that opinion. We shall, no doubt, be laughed at and derided on all sides, sneered at by friends who believe everything impracticable, and opposed by those malignant enemies who will be delighted to find an opportunity for manifesting their hostility. But no matter. We were derided and laughed at before by persons of this description when we set about the accomplishment of that great moral revolution which has won religious freedom for all."

These were brave words, bravely uttered, in defiance of the vast, intolerant, and unprincipled Opposition whose hostility and ridicule he had anticipated and defied. But they settled deep in the minds of those to whom they were addressed, and in time produced abundant fruits. Though during that and the two succeeding years the growth of the association was slow and not always regular, the opinions of the leaders in the movement were permeating the minds of the masses in every section of the country. O'Connell himself, by public letters, addresses, and private influence, was incessantly developing his plans and enforcing his arguments in favor of the absolute necessity of domestic legislation for Ireland. His speeches in Mullingar, Cork, Limerick, Belfast, and Carlow, during this period, were full of his ancient fire, vehemence, logic, and pathos, solidified and chastened by the experience of a long and laborious life. His election as Lord Mayor of Dublin in the latter part of 1841, not only drew to him the attention of the empire, but added a gravity and significance to his casual utterances far beyond what was attached to those of any other man of his nationality. He was now indeed the true leader of the Irish people, and around him crowded prelates, priests, and people—the old men who recollected the vanished glories of the days of Grattan and the volunteers, as well as the young spirits, fresh from their classic studies of Greek and Roman liberty, who knew nothing of the atrocities of '98 nor of the debasement of their fathers under the infamous persecutions that preceded and followed that sad catastrophe.

Among the latter were three men, comparatively young, who were destined to be among his most efficient supporters, so long as a sense of justice and a due regard for their country's welfare would allow them to be so. These were Thomas Davis, Charles Gavan Duffy, and John B. Dillon, the nucleus of what was afterwards called the "Young Ireland" party; and truly did they represent the young blood and young mind of Ireland, or rather the old spirit and ancient genius of their warrior ancestors rejuvenated and revivified. The first, Davis, was a Protestant, the other two, Catholics. Duffy had large experience as a journalist, Dillon was a lawyer, and Davis a man of letters. Each represented a province, north, west, and south, when they met in the capital of Leinster to establish a journal—*The Nation*—which, while designed to be devoted primarily to the advocacy of a repeal of the act of Union, was intended to create a national literature, a taste for Irish art and archæology, a love for Irish music and song, and to make them "racy of the soil."

The *Nation* was first issued in the autumn of 1842. Before many weeks had elapsed it had taken a position not only at the head of Irish journalism, but second to none of its class then published in any country or language. So solid, terse, and pointed were its editorials, so brilliant and captivating its literary essays and poetry, that in its very infancy it excited general astonishment and comment, and, with the magnetism of true genius, drew around it, proud to swell the tide of its fame, a host of volunteer contributors, some of whose names now are counted among those of the best writers of our century.

Of the three originators of this great

journal, THOMAS DAVIS was undoubtedly the most versatile, and, as a *littérateur*, the most gifted. Born in Mallow, in the county of Cork, A. D. 1814, he early imbibed the poetic *afflatus* which seems to delight in lingering round the mountains and babbling in the brooks of Munster. Not belonging to the proscribed faith, he had every advantage of a good education, and while still a youth entered the Dublin University. His life in Trinity was marked neither by incident nor any great signs of precocious ability. He passed through the regular course of study in the usual manner, without particular notice or remark, and went into the wide world with no apparent aim or definite course in life. He had, in fact, one of those peculiarly constituted minds, usually of slow development, which, unconscious of its own grasp and power, fails at first to see the straight path before it. His studies in college were systematically and conscientiously attended to, but he had no taste for the forms and fetters of pedantic scholasticism. He loved nature in all her bloom and freshness, and his happiest hours were devoted to the contemplation of her beauties or to communing with poets and naturalists who had exhausted their powers of description in her praise. Thus dreaming and aimless he passed the first years of his manhood. "During his college-course," says an intimate friend and fellow-student, "and for some years after, while he was very generally liked, he had, unless perhaps with some few who knew him intimately, but a moderate reputation for high ability of any kind."

At length Davis, in his twenty-eighth year, found his true vocation. Then his soul burst out in a gush of melody, and in strong, thrilling prose that captivated all hearts and carried conviction with them, such as mere oratory or ordinary verse could never have accomplished. Week after week the columns of the *Nation* were filled with his contributions on every conceivable subject affecting Ireland: her history, resources, literature, antiquities, and art; and with a plenitude of ideas and language, combined with such perfect mastery of his theme, that he astonished not only his associates but himself. The rock had been struck at last, and a pure, limpid stream of erudition and patriotism came forth to quench the ardent thirst for knowledge of his captive people. While he lived he was the life and soul of the Young Irelanders, their prophet and their guide, and though seldom found on the rostrum, he was admitted by all to be one of the principal, if not the very ablest, of the supporters of O'Connell.

It is, however, as a poet, as the one who had discovered the secret springs of the Irish character and knew well how to touch each in turn, that his memory is embalmed in the popular heart. Of all the brilliant spirits that added grace and harmony to the Repeal epoch, there is none so fondly remembered as he; for his ballads and songs have not only a local interest and a definite object attached to them, but they are so warm, so true to nature, and so consonant with Irish feeling that, heard but once or twice, they are sure never to be forgotten. When we reflect that only such moments as he could snatch from more serious occupations were devoted to the muses; that his selected poems as published fill a good sized volume; that, though many of them bear evidence of haste, they are every one full of deep and original thought, in most instances melodiously expressed; we are inclined to wonder at his previous silence as well as to speculate on what he might have produced had his life been prolonged for a few more years.

But our surprise is still further increased when we read, in the Introduction to his poems written by his friend Mr. Wallis, the following statement. "Until about three years before his death," this editor says, "I am assured he had never written a line of poetry. His efforts to acquire knowledge, to make himself useful, to find a suitable sphere of action, were incessant; but they tried every path, and took every direction but this. The warmth of his affections, and his intense enjoyment of the beauties of nature and character, literature and art, ought early to have marked him out as one destined to soar and sing, as well as to think and act. But the fact is, that among his youthful contemporaries, for many a long year, he got as little credit for any promise this way as he did for any other remarkable qualities, beyond extreme good-nature, untiring industry, and very varied learning." To this Mr. John Mitchel adds his testimony. "He was no boy-rhymer," he says, in his preface to the same collection, "and brimful as his eye and soul were of the beauties and glories of nature, he never felt a necessity to utter them in song."

That Davis, while doubtful of his own ability to supply the deficiency, was yet fully alive to the importance of song as a lever to raise a down-trodden race to manliness and independence, we are well assured by his own words. In his essay on the "Ballad Poetry of Ireland" he wrote: "That a country is without national poetry proves its hopeless dulness or its utter provincialism. National poetry is the very flowering of the soul—the greatest evidence of its health, the greatest excellence of its beauty. Its melody is balsam to the senses. It is the playfellow of childhood, ripens into the companion of his manhood, consoles his age. It presents the most dramatic events, the largest characters, the most impressive scenes, and the deepest passions in the language most familiar to us. It shows us magnified, and ennobles our hearts, our intellects, our country, and our countrymen —binds us to the past by its condensed and gem-like history, to the future by examples and by aspirations. It solaces us in travel, fires us in action, prompts our invention, sheds a grace beyond the power of luxury around our homes, is the recognized envoy of our minds among all mankind and to all time."

Inspired by such profound appreciation of the value of poetry, ballad, and song, in the education and elevation of the people, Davis wrote continually and always to the point, with steadily increasing excellence; and, if we have to-day in the English language melodies and ballads that no thorough Irishman need blush to sing or feel humiliated in hearing repeated, we owe it, in great part, to his pure genius and burning patriotism.

But alas! in the very hour of his greatest usefulness, while an entranced country hung lovingly on his notes, when on the very threshold of his fame, he was snatched away from his race and nation, to the deep regret of all, even of those who either would not or could not agree with his political or personal views. He died after a short sickness on the 16th of September, 1845, in Dublin, and was buried amid tears and lamentations in Mount Jerome church-yard outside of that city.

To those who know his worth, abilities, and character only through his writings, he stands forth as a noble, sagacious, and accomplished journalist; a pure-souled and unselfish patriot; a true poet, full of sublime aspirations and beautiful conceptions, wanting only the hand of time to mellow and retouch the defects of an untrained and exuberant fancy. But it is not always well to judge a man by his words or writings. Let us see, then, what some of his contemporaries and most intimate acquaintances—men who knew every pulsation of his heart and marked his every action—said of him. And first we take the opinion of the great Agitator. He was at Derrynane when the sad news reached him of the death of the young poet. He immediately wrote to the Repeal Association a letter, in which the following feeling allusions were made to the recent calamity.

"I do not know what to write. My mind is bewildered and my heart afflicted. The loss of my beloved friend—my noble-minded friend—is a source of the deepest sorrow to my mind. What a blow—what a cruel blow—to the cause of Irish nationality! He was a creature of transcendent qualities of mind and heart. His learning was universal—his knowledge was as minute as it was general. And then he was a being of such incessant energy and continuous exertion. I, of course, in the few years—if years they be—still left to me, cannot expect to look upon his like again or to see the place he has left vacant adequately filled up. And I solemnly declare that I never knew any man who could be so useful to Ireland in the present stage of her struggles. His loss is indeed irreparable. What an example he was to the Protestant youths of Ireland! What a noble emulation of his virtues ought to be excited in the Catholic young men of Ireland! And his heart, too!—it was as gentle, as kind, as loving as a woman's. Yes! it was as tenderly kind as his judgment was comprehensive and his genius magnificent. We shall long deplore his loss. As I stand alone in the solitude of my mountains, many a tear shall I shed to the memory of the noble youth. Oh! how vain are words or tears when such a national calamity afflicts the country. Put me down among the foremost contributors to whatever monument or tribute to his memory shall be voted by the National Association. Never did they perform a more imperative or—alas!—so sad a duty. I can write no more—my tears blind me; and after all, 'Fungar inane munere.'"

Charles Gavan Duffy, in writing shortly after the death of his lost co-laborer, said of him: "We are still too near to estimate his proportions truly. The friends to whom his singularly noble and lovable character was familiar, and who knew all the great designs he was bringing to maturity, are in no fit condition to measure his intellectual force with a calm judgment. The people who knew him imperfectly, or not at all—

for it was one of the practical lessons he taught the young men of his generation, to be chary of notoriety—have still to gather from his works whatever faint image of a truly great man can ever be collected from books. Till they have done this, they will not be prepared to hear the whole truth of him. All he was, and might have become, they can never fully know; as it is, their unconsciousness of what they have lost, impresses those who knew him with that pitying pain we feel for the indifference of a child to the death of his father. Students who will be eager to estimate him for themselves, must take in connection with his works the fact, that over the grave of this man, living only to manhood, and occupying only a private station, there gathered a union of parties and a combination of intellect that would have met round the tomb of no other man who has lived in our time. No life—not that of Guttenberg, or Franklin, or Tone—illustrates more strikingly than his, how often it is necessary to turn aside from the *dais* on which stand the great and titled, for the great moving power of the time—the men who are stirring like a soul in the bosom of society. Such a one they will quickly discover Davis to have been."

The late General Thomas Francis Meagher, one of Davis's earliest pupils, and always his warm admirer, spoke of him in his wonted glowing and impassioned terms of admiration. Alluding to the attempts to heal differences which had sprung up between the members of the Association shortly previous to the poet's decease, he thus said: "Amid the discordant elements, the heart and voice and pen of Thomas Davis were tasked to the uttermost to restore union, cordiality, and brotherly love. Never did genius or truth assert a brighter future than when she flashed from his pen in the din of these unnatural passions. . . The death of Thomas Davis was an unspeakable calamity. Never did heavier one fall on a doomed nation." John Mitchel, his successor on the *Nation*, also adds his tribute to the worth and genius of his predecessor:

"By his ardent temperament," he writes, "amiable character, and high accomplishments, he soon gathered around him a gifted circle of educated young men, Protestant and Catholic, whose head-quarters was the *Nation* office, and whose chief bond of union was their warm attachment to their friend. It was the one grand object of these men— and it was grand—to lift up the Irish cause high above Catholic claims and Protestant pretensions, to unite all sects in the one character of 'Irishmen,' to put an end to English domination. Their idea was precisely the idea of the United Irishmen; although their mode of action was very different."

In reading over these eloquent eulogies we can form some idea of the loss which the country sustained in the death of Davis at the critical moment when the action of the Repeal Association was paralyzed by internal dissensions, and the shadow of the impending famine was already casting its gloom over the face of the land. But, as it has been well said, they never fail who die in a good cause. We have still with us those brilliant coruscations of his genius which will shine like meteors on the onward path of future laborers in the field in which he wrought so well, and for which he, in his short life, accomplished so much good.

CHAPTER III.

The Repeal year—Monster meetings—The Nation—Opening of Conciliation Hall—William Smith O'Brien—His birth and descent—Career in parliament—Joins the Repeal Association.

AFTER nearly three years spent in preparation, O'Connell felt that the time had come to arouse the entire country, and to force on the people of England and Scotland and, indeed, on all Christendom, the conviction that at least four-fifths of the Irish were thoroughly unanimous in their demands for the restoration of their parliament; and were resolved that their voice should be heard on this all-important subject by friends and foes alike. The mode of proceeding which he proposed to himself was the holding of vast, open-air meetings in different portions of the provinces, to the end that the entire population of the country might have a full opportunity of hearing the repeal question fully discussed in all its bearings; and, by their multitudinous presence of indorsing the actions of their representatives in the imperial legislature. The voice of a united and (being united), powerful nation, demanding rights at once just and expedient to be granted, could not, he argued, be raised in vain.

Accordingly, early in 1843, from his home in Derrynane, he addressed a letter to the Association requiring that three million repealers should be enrolled, which being done, he promised that the Irish parliament would be restored. But he was not content to leave this work altogether to the committee, and the repeal wardens. He resolved to forego his attendance on the coming session of parliament, and to devote his entire time and energy to arousing the people.

He therefore left his home, in January, for Dublin, where he intended to strike the first blow, in the capital and in the presence of the highest representative body of the country. He had already put on the books of the corporation a notice of motion declaring the necessity of a repeal of the Union act. The debate on this motion took place in the Assembly Rooms, on the 28th of February and occupied three days, amid intense excitement. O'Connell opened the proceedings by presenting the following propositions, and supported them in a speech of remarkable power, calmness, and familiarity with the subject. They were: "1st, The capability and capacity of the Irish nation for an independent legislature. 2d, The perfect right of Ireland to have a domestic parliament. 3d, This right was fully established by the transactions of 1782. 4th, That the most beneficial effects accrued to Ireland from her parliamentary independence. 5th, That the Irish parliament was utterly incompetent to annihilate the Irish Constitution by uniting with England. 6th, That as the Union was carried by fraud, force, terror, and the grossest corruption, it is not a bargain or contract. 7th, That the most disastrous consequences resulted to Ireland from the Union. 8th, That the Union can be abolished by peaceable and constitutional means—without the violation of law and without the destruction of property or life. 9th, That none but the most salutary results can spring from a repeal of the Union."

He was answered at great length and with marked ability by Mr. Isaac Butt, Q. C., now one of the leaders of the Home-Rule movement, and even then a quasi-repealer, though the spokesman of the Tory aldermen. All the arguments that keen, legal ingenuity could devise and finished elocution express, were advanced and reiterated against O'Connell's propositions, but with little effect on the corporators, and none at all on the audience. The Emancipator closed the debate in his happiest style. "No report," says one who was present, "no description could possibly do justice to that magnificent reply. O'Connell took up in succession all the objections of his opponents, and demolished them one by one. The whole phalanx of Unionists looked like pygmies in the grasp of a giant. The dexterities of Butt—some of which had been plausibly managed—shrank and withered into nothing when touched by O'Connell. The consciousness of a great moral triumph seemed to animate his voice —his glance—his gestures. Never had I heard him so eloquent; never had I witnessed so noble a display of his transcendent powers." The victory was complete, and the resolution was carried by a vote of forty-one against fifteen. The key-note, thus struck, reverberated throughout the island, and the corporations of the various cities hastened to take it up and swell the chorus for repeal.

This was but a prelude, however, to what were, with justice, called the "monster meetings." The first of these was held at Trim on the 16th of March, 1843, and at the banquet which followed it O'Connell uttered the memorable apothegms: "Better to die like a freeman than be sold like a slave; . . . it will not do to say you like to be free. What care I for your liking it, if you do not reduce it into action? The man who thinks and does not act upon his thoughts is a scoundrel who does not deserve to be free." Then followed similar gatherings at Cahirconlish, Bellewstown, Clones, Rathkeale, and Limerick; at the latter place over a hundred thousand persons of all ages, sexes, and conditions turned out to receive him, and a few days after he met nearly double that number at Kells. On the 14th of May was held the great meeting of Mullingar, of which O'Connell, afterwards speaking before the Association, said: "I do not exaggerate my belief that there were hundreds of thousands assembled at that meeting. It was a majestic assembly of sober, loyal, patriotic people. The number of Catholic clergymen that attended there—the talent they displayed—the anxiety they exhibited, made it still more important; and then there were two bishops of the Catholic Church at the head of the meeting."

The prelates thus alluded to were the Most Rev. Dr. Cantwell, the patriotic Archbishop of Meath, and Dr. Higgins, Bishop of Ardagh, the latter of whom, in the course of a most glowing speech, said:

"I wish to state that I have every reason to believe—I may add that I *know*, that every Catholic bishop in Ireland, without exception, is an ardent Repealer. I know that virtually you all have reason to believe that the bishops of Ireland are repealers; but I have now again formally to announce to you that they have all declared themselves as such, and that from shore to shore we are repealers. I, for one, defy all the ministers of England to put down the agitation in the diocese of Ardagh. If they attempt, my friends, to rob us of the daylight, which is I believe, common to all, and prevent us from assembling in the open fields, we will retire to our chapels, and we shall suspend all other instruction in order to devote all our time to teaching the people to be Repealers in spite of them. If they beset our temples and mix spies with our people, we shall prepare our people for the circumstances—if they bring us for that to the scaffold, in dying for the cause of our country, we shall bequeath our wrongs to our successors."

The allusion in Bishop Higgins's address to the possibility of coercive measures being resorted to, was called out by the declaration of Sir Robert Peel, the English prime minister, in response to a question in the House of Commons, that "there is no influence, no power, no authority which the prerogative of the crown or the existing laws give the government, that shall not be exercised for the purpose of maintaining the Union—the dissolution of which would involve, not merely the repeal of an act of parliament, but the dismemberment of this great empire." He likewise stated the further threat that if the laws then on the statute book were not sufficient to suppress the Irish agitation, the ministry would apply to parliament for more effectual powers.

The challenge thus thrown down by Peel to the Irish people was quickly and joyously taken up, and instead of intimidating them added zest to their patriotism. The monster meetings became more frequent and more gigantic than ever. That of Charleville, May 18th, was attended by some three hundred thousand people; and on the 21st, half a million persons assembled at Cork to hear the Liberator speak, and to pass strong, earnest resolutions in favor of home government. Two days after he addressed four hundred thousand at Cashel, and on the 25th, an equal number at Nenagh. On the 28th, over a quarter of a million assembled at Longford; on the 4th of June, one hundred and fifty thousand met at Drogheda; four days subsequently there were three hundred thousand at Kilkenny; four hundred thousand at Mallow, on the 11th; seven hundred thousand in Clare on the 15th, and a hundred thousand at Athlone, the centre of Ireland, on the 16th of June.

Never was there more order, good-humor, or stern resolve exhibited in any nation or age than that which characterized those immense assemblages of unarmed men; and never did popular orator, warrior, or monarch in ancient or modern days appear before such numerous, obedient, and enthusiastic multitudes. The very name of O'Connell was a talisman that called together, on the shortest notice, hundreds of thousands, and though it was beyond the reach of possibility that any human being could be heard by one half of those assembled on such occasions, those who did not hear saw their darling chief, and went away contented to learn subsequently the gist of his words from their more fortunate neighbors.

The numbers who left their ordinary avocations and travelled for miles to attend those monster meetings were incredible, nor could we believe them ourselves had we not personally witnessed two such gatherings. They were usually held in the vicinity of places where two or more roads intersected each other. From early dawn of the eventful day of such a meeting might be seen throngs of men of all ranks in life trooping along the roads, converging on the *point d'appui*. The rural districts gave forth thousands of stalworth farmers, well mounted, and myriads of hardy tillers of the soil on foot; while the villages and towns sent out their various trades, under proper leaders, with the banners and other appropriate insignia of their guilds. Bands of music, generally furnished by the local temperance societies, were interspersed in the various tributary processions, and on the pure morning breeze floated the stirring notes of many a martial or patriotic air. As each detachment arrived it was assigned its proper place on the field with something like military order; the cavalry, or rather the cavalcades, on the flanks, and the footmen in the centre, till a complete semi-disk was formed in front of the platform. Though thirty years have passed we almost imagine we can once more behold the grand spectacle. There is a pause: a cloud of dust is seen in the far distance, and a cheer from those nearest to it announces that it is the carriage of the Liberator. The shout is taken up along the line, again and again repeated. The carriages halt at the rear of the platform, and O'Connell and his staff ascend, the numerous bands playing a welcome. The chairman gets up to open the meeting, but he is scarcely heard or heeded. At last a majestic figure comes forward, and, doffing his cap, bows low to the multitude amid a storm, a very hurricane of applause. His presence alone is a speech; in his eye there is the eloquence of a hundred orators; his port is the sublime impersonation of grandeur and power. He stands indeed the " uncrowned monarch of the Irish people"; and never had king or kaiser more devoted subjects.

At length he is allowed to speak; and his stentorian tones roll over the heads of that sea of human beings like a roll of thunder or the voice of the storm, till even the very hills take them up and send them back again. Those who are fortunately nearest to him, strain every nerve to drink in each word he says; those far beyond ear-shot are content to rivet their gaze on that ponderous face, and guess, from its varied expression, the meaning of what he is saying. But though tens and hundreds of thousands, from different parishes, baronies, and even counties, are assembled, all is order, peace, and the best of feelings; and when the meeting is over they disperse. Each goes to his home, full of enthusiasm and hope for his native land.

With wonderful energy O'Connell continued his series of assemblies into the early autumn. In the latter part of June, and the months of July and August, meetings were held at Dundalk, Skibbereen, Galway, Donnybrook, Waterford, Tullamore, Wexford, Tuam, Mayo, Clontibret, and other central localities, at which, it was estimated, at least three millions of people, collectively, attended. At the historic hill of Tara, on the 15th of August, another demonstration of surpassing sublimity was made. "Nearly every district in Ireland," writes a biographer of O'Connell, "sent its tributaries to this great ocean of human life. The meeting was enlivened by forty-two bands of music, some of which had travelled a distance of over fifty miles. During the whole preceding night crowds were constantly arriving, and at the dawn of day the grass-grown hill, clothed in perpetual verdure—where St. Patrick converted kings and the United Irishmen fought for the freedom of Ireland—was mantled with men —black with human swarms. Nothing else could be seen. O'Connell's carriage, slowly wading through this dense mass, consumed two hours in accomplishing one mile. As he approached the hill he could see a priest on the very summit, standing before a temporary altar, celebrating the divine mysteries, at which seven hundred thousand people knelt and prayed. When the Masses, which continued from nine till twelve, were all ended, a priest preached a sermon on temperance, and, raising his hands, invoked the blessing of heaven on the bending thousands and on their Liberator."

At the last of these great popular gatherings, which took place at Mullaghmast in the following October, an incident occurred which, though peaceful and harmless in itself, was full of significance to the English authorities, and doubtless had a great influence on their subsequent dealings with the repeal leaders. Nearly half a million people were surrounding the platform upon which was seated the Liberator in all the plenitude of his power, and with a dignity that his long and hitherto successful struggles with the oppressor had added to his naturally noble form and reverend old age. Suddenly there emerged from the crowd of distinguished gentlemen on the stand, no less a personage than the sculptor Hogan, who advancing toward O'Connell, placed on his head a cap of green velvet embroidered with gold, and designed after the fashion of an ancient Irish crown. "Sir," said the donor, when the wild applause of the meeting had subsided, "my only regret is that this is not of gold." The Liberator in reply said, in his most impressive manner, "I shall wear this cap with the proud remembrance that it was given to me on the Rath of Mullaghmast, and that it was placed upon my head by one of the first of modern sculptors in this or any country. I shall continue to wear it during my life, and it shall afterwards be buried with me in my grave."

This meeting may be called the culmination of the Repeal movement; much that followed was downward, hopeless, and full of misery and national humiliation.

It having been agreed between the leaders in the Association that the out-door agitation for the year should be closed by a grand rally to surpass all preceding ones, the plains of Clontarf, outside Dublin, sacred in Ireland's history as the scene of the utter defeat of the Danish invaders by the illustrious Brian, and the spot upon which that great warrior and statesman died, Sunday, the 8th of October, was selected as the day; but long before its arrival the metropolis was crowded with deputations from the principal cities and towns, and visitors not only from the remotest parts of the island, but from England, Scotland, and the Continent. The Castle authorities, alarmed at the previous impressive demonstrations, resolved at all hazards to prevent the intended assemblage, and took such insidious steps to carry out their plans, as led to the very grave suspicion that they intended, if opportunity offered, a general massacre of the defenceless people.

Though the day and place of meeting were known to every one weeks before, it was only on the 7th, the day previous to the one selected by the Repealers, that the intention of the government was made manifest. Late on the evening of Saturday, when it was too dark for the passers-by to read, a proclamation was posted on the city walls, signed by the Lord-Lieutenant, De Grey, prohibiting the meeting. At the same time the roads leading from all directions into Dublin were thronged by ardent and enthusiastic repealers, who hoped that the next morning would bring them face to face with the much loved Chieftain, who then held the destiny of their country in his hands. It was impossible that those numberless thousands could be informed of the proclamation or intercepted in their march and prevented from encamping overnight on the ground, except extraordinary efforts were made to apprise them of the villanous plans of the government. The Repeal Committee hastily met, O'Connell at its head, and resolved, even at that late moment, to frustrate the diabolical designs of their enemies by postponing the meeting. As quickly as possible the public were informed of this determination by a counter proclamation signed by O'Connell; and messengers, well mounted, were despatched in every direction along the road, to turn back the hosts who were concentrating on the capital.

At the time, and some years after, the wisdom and expediency of this decision of the committee were very seriously doubted by men of large intelligence and warm national feeling; but in the light of the experience of more than a quarter of a century we think that to have attempted a meeting on that occasion would have been an act of gross cruelty and inhumanity. The assembled people would have been, to a man, unarmed, while the government was fully prepared. Of cavalry, artillery, and infantry it had abundance, in fact a very respectable army, well drilled, officered, and equipped; the guns of the Pigeon House fort covered the approaches to Clontarf, while three ships of war in the harbor ran out their guns to enfilade the very place of the expected meeting. Had a contrary policy been pursued than that suggested by O'Connell, the result would have been, beyond any doubt, a most relentless and merciless slaughter of the defenceless patriots, to which the very magnitude, and density of their ranks would have contributed additional horror. Fortunately, the meeting did not take place, and the repeal cause was greatly the gainer thereby.

During all the commotion of the memorable repeal year, the *Nation* fairly glittered with arguments in favor of the movement, and irresistible appeals to the people to rise up and assert their rights to self-government. O'Connell never had so useful an ally as this potent newspaper, the product of a hundred gifted, energetic, and accomplished minds: and, though he sometimes thought its tone too revolutionary, he gladly accepted the services, and freely recognized the ability and sincerity of its conductors. The plain, straightforward, and overpowering logic of Duffy; the brilliant, vehement prose and poetry of Davis, and the multitudinous and ever-varying essays and poems of a host of contributors, all concentrated in one journal and on one object, could not be resisted by Irish hearts. The efforts of the *Nation*, which were ever directed to heal all dissensions among Irishmen of different forms of faith, and to unite

Catholics and Protestants under the one banner, were about this time particularly successful; and its friends were deeply gratified by the adhesion of a gentleman who was destined to occupy a very prominent position in the subsequent struggles for repeal.

On the 22d of October, 1843, the new building erected by the Association, called Conciliation Hall, was formally opened. Though very spacious it was filled to overflowing. Many prominent gentlemen presented themselves, and letters of congratulation and sympathy were read from Lord French, Sir C. Wolesley, Sir R. Musgrave, and others. But what created the most intense satisfaction was a communication from WILLIAM S. O'BRIEN, M. P. for Limerick, announcing his adhesion to the cause of the repeal of the Union. A portion of that letter read as follows:

"Lest I should be led to form a precipitate decision, I availed myself of the interval which followed the close of the session, to examine whether, among the Governments of Central Europe, there are any so indifferent to the interests of their subjects as England has been to the welfare and happiness of our population. After visiting Belgium, and all the principal capitals of Germany I returned home impressed with the sad conviction that there is more human misery in one county in Ireland, than throughout all the populous cities and districts which I had visited. On landing in England I learn that the Ministry, instead of applying themselves to remove the causes of complaint, have resolved to deprive us even of the liberty of discontent—that public meetings are to be suppressed—and that state prosecutions are to be carried on against Mr. O'Connell, and others, on some frivolous charges of sedition and conspiracy.

"I should be unworthy to belong to a nation which may claim, at least as a characteristic virtue, that it exhibits increased fidelity in the hour of danger, if I were to delay any longer to dedicate myself to the cause of my country. Slowly, reluctantly convinced that Ireland has nothing to hope from the sagacity, the justice, or the generosity of the English parliament, my reliance shall henceforth be placed upon our own native energy and patriotism."

When O'Brien resolved to cast his lot with the national party he was in the prime of his manhood and in the full enjoyment of his mental faculties. Having been born in Clare on the 17th day of October, 1803, he had just completed his fortieth year, and though educated at Harrow and Cambridge, where English prejudices prevailed to their fullest extent, his mind, while absorbing all the knowledge afforded in these institutions, never for a moment entertained a feeling but those of proud love for his native land and a yearning sympathy for her manifold sufferings. Descended from the princely house of Thomond, whose ancestors can be traced in an uninterrupted line, from the great Brian Boromha, he was by nature and by blood a patriot. His grandfather, Sir Lucius O'Brien, who had long been a member of the Irish parliament, was noted for his independence and unflinching honesty; and his father, Sir Edward O'Brien, who sat in the same body during its latter years, was one of the stanchest and most incorruptible of the anti-Union party.

Mr. W. S. O'Brien entered the imperial parliament for the borough of Ennis when in his twenty-fifth year, and in 1832 he was elected by the voters of the county of Limerick one of their representatives, a position he continued to hold until 1849, when his seat was declared vacant. He commenced public life as a moderate Whig, but from the first he considered the interests of his country paramount to all party considerations. In 1829, when O'Connell stood for Clare a second time, O'Brien issued an address to the people of his native county, in which he endeavored, but without effect, to dissuade them from supporting the Emancipator. "Mr. O'Connell," he wrote, "endeavors to delude those among you who know little of political matters, by representing himself as the sole author of the emancipation of the Catholics. When you hear these extravagant pretensions, you should be informed that it has long been a question with the most attentive observers of the progress of that measure, whether his intemperance has not been the chief cause of its delay; and that of the majorities that carried it through, more than four-fifths were English representatives, wholly beyond the reach of any influence, except the justice of the cause—and that all were Protestants."

The first statement in this paragraph manifestly is an error; the two latter are facts very capable of elucidation. More than four-fifths of the law-makers for Ireland unfortunately are Englishmen who hold themselves "wholly beyond the reach of an influence" which millions of the Irish people —composing it is said an integral portion of the British empire—are unable to bring to bear on them, hence the strongest argument in favor of a repeal of the Union. That the Emancipation act was carried by Protestant votes arose from the very good reason that at the time none but Protestants were allowed to sit in parliament.

Mr. O'Connell's reply to O'Brien was forcible and convincing; but being altogether too personal, and so tinged with unfounded aspersions on the family of his opponent, much of its moral effect was lost on the public. O'Brien had also asserted that none of the gentry of Clare supported the Emancipation candidate; and this expression having excited the ire of the O'Gorman Mahon and Mr. Steele, who were natives of the county, the latter challenged him to mortal combat, the former acting as his second. A duel was the consequence, in which shots were exchanged; but happily neither of the principals was injured, and the matter was amicably settled. Mr. Mahon in turn sent a hostile message to O'Brien, but upon his explaining that the words to which exception had been taken were not intended for him, that matter was allowed to drop.

Still O'Brien in parliament continued to hold a position of neutrality, and semi-independence of the existing parties, without being looked upon as belonging to the Nationalists. Time, however, was slowly but surely bringing to him the sad conviction that no justice could be expected from English politicians. He was insensibly gravitating toward the great mass of his countrymen, even in spite of his early impressions. In May, 1843, when Lord Chancellor Sir Edward Sugden dismissed all the repeal magistrates, he resigned his commission, and in a manly letter to Sugden he said that though not a repealer he could not consent to hold so important an office upon such disgraceful conditions.

Soon after, while the parliament was going through the forms of a discussion on the disarming act, O'Brien rose from his seat, and to the amazement of both Whigs and Conservatives, moved that the House, in place of passing so cruel and unjustifiable a measure, should resolve itself in a committee of the whole to inquire into the actual condition of Ireland. His speech on that occasion, July 4th, is said to have been even more than usually grave, impressive, and replete with a knowledge of the resources, wants, and miseries of the Irish people. Mr. Mitchell thus epitomizes it in his "History of Ireland": "He pointed out the facts which justified discontent—that the union made Ireland poor and kept her poor—that it encouraged the absenteeism and so caused a great rental to be spent in England—that, nearly a million sterling of 'surplus revenue,' over what was expended in the government of Ireland was annually remitted from the

Irish to the English exchequer—that Irish manufactures had ceased, and the profits of all the manufactured articles consumed in that island came to England—that the tenantry had no permanent tenure or security that they would derive benefit by any improvements they might make—that Ireland had but one hundred and five members of parliament, whereas her population and revenue together entitled her to one hundred and seventy-five—that the municipal laws of the two countries were not the same—then the new 'Poor Law' was a failure, and was increasing the wretchedness and hunger of the people—and the right honorable gentleman (Sir R. Peel) had now declared his ultimatum; he had declared that 'conciliation had reached its limits'; and that the Irish should have an Arms bill, and nothing but an Arms bill."

The motion so ably advocated was lost, the Disarming bill was passed into a law by overwhelming majorities; and O'Brien, despairing of any good from alien legislation, and acting upon most deliberate conviction, determined to devote the balance of his life to the advocacy of domestic government. In a popular point of view, particularly in the south, where he was well known and, personally, much respected, this decisive step was a source of deep congratulation to the repealers; but it was as the representative of an ancient and most illustrious line, as a landholder and a Protestant, that his presence was most welcomed by the leaders of the movement. Of thorough education, rare personal honor and courage, and of stainless character, he brought to the Association a varied practical knowledge of the different systems of European governments and nearly twenty years' experience acquired as an indefatigable and observant parliamentarian.

CHAPTER IV.

Arrest of O'Connell, John O'Connell, Duffy, Gray, Barrett, Ray, Steele, Rev. Fathers Tyrrell and Tierney—The feeling of the country—State trials—Conviction—Effect in Parliament—Sentence and imprisonment—More troops for Ireland—Reversal of the judgment—General rejoicing.

On the 14th of October, 1843, O'Connell and a number of his most prominent associates were arrested and held to bail on charges of entering into a conspiracy to intimidate the government, to supersede the tribunals of justice, and other divers seditious practices too numerous to mention; all, however, subsequently set out on a roll of parchment ninety-seven feet long, being the indictment, which was found by a Dublin grand-jury January 15th, 1844. The names mentioned in that formidable document were, Daniel O'Connell, M. P. for Cork; his son, John O'Connell, M. P. for Kilkenny; Charles Gavan Duffy, editor of the *Nation*; Richard Barrett, editor of the *Pilot*; Dr.

(now Sir John) Grey, editor of the *Freeman's Journal;* Thomas Matthew Ray, secretary of the Association; Rev. Mr. Tierney, of Clontibret, county Monaghan; and Thomas Steele. The Rev. Mr. Tyrrell, of Lusk, county Dublin, though arrested with the others, died soon after from sickness superinduced by the extraordinary exertions he had used on the eve of the intended meeting at Clontarf.

The prompt obedience of the people to the behests of the repeal committee in deciding to postpone that gathering had so much of military discipline in it, and showed so completely how thoroughly O'Connell held them in hand, that it is questionable whether the step taken by the authorities was not a blunder as much as, if persisted in, it would have been a monstrous crime. And now, when the repealers saw their trusted and faithful leaders entangled in the meshes of the law, and that law administered in the interest of their implacable enemies, by corrupt or weak-minded judges, sheriffs appointed by the crown for their subserviency and total absence of conscience, and packed juries carefully selected not to try, but to convict; their conduct was admirable. Nothing intimidated or disheartened, they set to work more earnestly than ever to recruit the repeal ranks. The greatest excitement, no doubt, prevailed throughout the island, but all was peace and order, and money flowed freely into the exchequer of Conciliation Hall, to be used in the propagation of the cause and in defence of the menaced leaders. Every Monday the large hall of the Association was crowded by members of parliament, private and professional gentlemen of fortune and eminence, the stalworth farmers of the provinces and the most respectable merchants and traders of the metropolis.

The trial itself lasted till the second week in February, but though the deepest interest was taken in its proceedings, no one was astonished at the result; for even before its commencement it was generally understood that the jury was to be packed; that all the Catholics and liberal Protestants were to be stricken off the array, and the good name, liberty, and property of the accused, left to the tender mercies of the Orangemen. "If our Saviour himself were in the dock," Jack Giffard, a notorious Orange juryman, is reported to have said, "the Dublin Orangemen would find him guilty to serve their party." O'Connell and his son were defended by Richard Lalor Sheil, the eloquent assistant of the Liberator during the emancipation struggle; while the other defendants were represented by Whiteside, Fitzgibbon, Henn, and Macdonagh—all lawyers of great experience and legal acumen.

From the beginning O'Connell resolved to take part in the defence. He could not let slip such a favorable opportunity to dilate on his favorite theme, nor was it often that he could find so peculiar an audience or have his words spread so correctly and extensively before the world. On the nineteenth day of the trial he rose and addressed the jury in terms which, though often eloquent and frequently impassioned, were more remarkable for their dignity, calmness, and solidity of logic. He ignored the smaller and more technical points of the counsel on both sides, and confined himself to two questions: that no conspiracy had been formed, or attempted to be proved, that the present proceeding was illegal and unjustifiable, and therefore unlawful and unconstitutional. In reference to the former he said to the jury:

"It is quite certain that there are considerable discrepancies of opinion between you and me, on subjects of the utmost importance; you differ with me on the question of the Repeal of the Union—for if you did not, there is not one of you would be in that box; you differ with me on a more important subject, in religious belief—for if you did not, you would not be in that box. These differences are perhaps aggravated by the fact that I am not only a Catholic, but that Catholic who (without boasting) has done most to pull down that Protestant ascendency for which perhaps you were the champions, but certainly not the antagonists; and although having established that equality, against which some of you contend and against which all your opinions were formed, it does not terrify me from the performance of my duty; for—I care not what evil effects occur to myself or what punishment it may bring on me—I glory in what I have done—I glory that I have been the successful and you the beaten party. But, gentlemen, nevertheless, I trust in your honor and sincerity; and to that alone I appeal. . . . I leave the case in your hands. I deny that I have done anything to stain me. I reject with contempt the appellation of conspirator. I have acted boldly in open day, in the presence of the magistracy; there has been nothing secret or concealed. I have struggled for the restoration of the parliament of my native country. Others have succeeded before me; but succeed or fail, it was a struggle to make the fairest land in the world possess those benefits which nature intended she should enjoy."

In the House of Commons the news of the conviction of the "conspirators" created great commotion. The Whigs were out of power and the Tories were tottering to a fall, so that the spokesmen of the former, like Macaulay, Russell, and others, with a keen eye to a restoration, found in the trial a powerful weapon against their opponents. Lord Russell, in giving a history of the proceedings in a speech of several hours' duration, made use of the following remarkable words, which are here quoted as the deliberate testimony of one of the most anti-

Irish and anti-Catholic statesmen that ever sat in either house of parliament. He said:

"Nominally, indeed, the two countries have the same laws. Trial by jury, for instance, exists in both countries; but is it administered alike in both? Sir, I remember on one occasion when an honorable gentleman (Mr. Brougham), on bringing forward a motion, in 1823, on the administration of the law in Ireland, made use of these words: 'The law of England esteemed all men equal. It was sufficient to be born within the king's allegiance to be entitled to all the rights the loftiest subject of the land enjoyed. None were disqualified; the only distinction was between natural born subjects and aliens. Such indeed was the liberality of our system in the times which we called barbarous, but from which, in these enlightened days, it might have been well to take a hint, that if a man were even an alien born, he was not deprived of the protection of the law. In Ireland, however, the law held a directly opposite doctrine. The sect to which a man belonged, the cast of his religious opinions, the form in which he worshipped his Creator, were grounds upon which the law separated him from his fellows, and bound him to the endurance of a system of the most cruel injustice.' Such was the statement of Mr. Brougham when he was the advocate of the oppressed. But, sir, let me ask, was what I have just now read the statement of a man who was ignorant of the country of which he spoke? No; the same language or to the same effect, was used by Sir M. O'Loughlin, in his evidence before the House of Lords. That gentleman stated that he had been in the habit of going the Munster circuit for nineteen years, and on that circuit it was the general practice for the Crown, in criminal prosecutions, to set aside all Catholics and all the liberal Protestants; and he added that he had been informed that on other circuits the practice was carried on in a more strict manner. Sir M. O'Loughlin also mentioned one case of this kind which took place in 1834, during the lord-lieutenancy of the Marquis of Wellesley, and the attorney-generalship of Mr. Blackbourne, the present Master of the Rolls, and in which, out of forty-three persons set aside (in a cause which was not a political one) there were thirty-six Catholics and seven Protestants, all of them respectable men. This practice is so well known, and carried out so generally, that men known to be liberals, whether Catholics or Protestants, have ceased to attend assizes, that they might not be exposed to these public insults. Now, I would ask, are these proofs of equal laws, or laws equally administered? Could the same, or similar cases have happened in Yorkshire, or Sussex, or Kent? Are these the fulfilment of the promise made and engagements entered into at the Union?"

Such language as this from the leader of a great party, though even less than the truth, would at the time of utterance have astonished everybody had it not been felt that an English Whig is capable of saying or doing anything for the sake of office. Four short years were not allowed to pass when the very same crimes against justice, in a more aggravated form, were perpetrated by this party, and those very speakers who had once more regained power.

From the day of the arrest of the repeal leaders, troops were being constantly poured into the country; regiment after regiment was daily landed in Dublin or some of the neighboring ports; marching and countermarching were the order of the day, and the streets of the capital were in a perpetual state of excitement from the glittering of thousands of bayonets, the gleaming of sabres, and the heavy rumble of artillery and caissons. In October, there were in Ireland twenty-eight thousand regular troops, besides about ten thousand well-armed constabulary, and the remnant of the militia; in February following it was calculated that there were at least forty thousand soldiers in Dublin alone, or within a couple of days' march of it. And, as if this were not enough, the King of Hanover—a man black with every crime political and personal from murder downwards—was graciously pleased to offer the *loan* of twenty thousand men to her most gracious majesty to slaughter her most faithful subjects *à les Hessians*. The objects of the government were now perfectly patent—to provoke discontent by imprisoning the leaders; to drive the people, thus left without guides, into insurrection, and to enact the tragedy of '98 over again. The means which Pitt and Castlereagh adopted to insure the Union, it was supposed by Peel and De Gray, would prove equally effectual to perpetuate it.

On the 30th of May, 1844, nearly three months after conviction, the "conspirators" were brought up in the Queen's Bench for sentence. To O'Connell as the chief offender was awarded one year's imprisonment, a fine of £2,000, and the filing of a personal bond of £5,000, with two sureties justifying in £2,500 each, to keep the peace for seven years. Charles Gavan Duffy and the other traverser were to be imprisoned for nine months, fined each £50, and to enter into their own recognizance of £1,000, with two sureties of £500 each, to keep the peace for the same length of time. This was English justice—as then and now, and all the time administered in Ireland.

The conspirators against the peace of the realm were then safely lodged in Richmond penitentiary. Where now were the millions that rallied round them the previous year? Where the masses that greeted the Liberator at Mallow and Wexford, Tara and Mullaghmast, and cheered to the echo every word that fell from his lips savoring of freedom and independence? Surely they would rise in their might, and by the sheer force of numbers overwhelm their oppressors and drive them from the island. Not so. The dragoons, the artillery, and the "British grenadiers" sharpened their sabres, trained their guns and pipe-clayed their accoutrements in tranquillity. Even the bloody King of Hanover lost the opportunity of filling his depleted coffers from the common treasury of England and Ireland by selling the blood of his stolid subjects: for O'Connell, immediately after his imprisonment, wrote to the Irish people to be patient and to give the enemy no chance of revenge; and they obeyed him most faithfully. To a friend who had called on him in prison he remarked: "The people are behaving nobly. I was at first afraid, despite all my teaching, that at such a trying crisis they would have done either too much or too little— either have been stung into an outbreak— or awed into apathy. Neither has happened, blessed be God!—the people are acting nobly!"

The people did indeed exhibit remarkable forbearance and vitality. Had O'Connell and his friends but given the slightest encouragement for armed resistance and rescue, there cannot be the least doubt but both would have been cheerfully, nay, gladly attempted by millions of their devoted adherents; nor can the horrible result of such rash acts, if resorted to, be for a moment questioned. As it was, chafing under the double insult of packed juries and hireling soldiery, the people showed their attachment to their chiefs as well as their contempt for the troops, by thousands of local meetings and by pouring into the repeal treasury thousands of pounds sterling every week. A "prison fund," for the further defence of the incarcerated, was likewise established, while the citizens of Dublin flooded the jail with all sorts of presents for their joint personal comfort.

Meanwhile an appeal had been taken from the lower Court to the House of Lords. After a good deal of learned nonsense on the part of the noble members of that body, lay and clerical, the writ of error was referred to the law lords, Lyndhurst, Brougham (the same whom Russell had quoted!) Cottenham, Denman, and Campbell. The first two, being of the party in power, decided that the trial was in every respect conducted according to law and equity; the others, who were on the side of those out of office, while not passing on the guilt or innocence of the prisoners, declared the method of trying them contrary to law, and that they should be set at liberty.

This news reached Dublin on the 5th of September, and was spread through the island with wonderful rapidity. The people were intoxicated with joy, their enthusiasm knew no bounds, for they looked upon the reversal of the decision of the Orange jury and the corrupt judges, as another triumph for their invincible leader, and as the harbinger of new life for their country. Two days afterwards the formal procession from the Bridewell to O'Connell's house was arrayed at the former place, and after passing through the principal streets of the city halted at Merrion square. Half a million of people thronged the line of march; the houses, almost, without exception, were gayly decorated, and a spirit of enthusiasm and exaltation beyond description pervaded all ranks of society. From the balcony of his residence O'Connell addressed the surging multitude below. Alluding to the former monster meetings he said: "One meeting alone remained unassembled—the meeting of Clontarf. Some of the minions of power laid, I fear, a scheme to dye that day in gore—to deluge the soil with the blood of the people; but we disappointed them. I issued my counter proclamation and it was obeyed. The people did not put themselves in danger. But has the law since declared that we were acting illegally? Oh! no—it dared not do that; but it spelled illegality out of a number of legal meetings. Our Clontarf meeting has not taken place as yet, but it will be for the Repeal Association, which has the confidence of the Irish people, to determine whether it may not be necessary, for the sake of public principle, to decide whether that meeting may not be hereafter held. I hope they may arrive at the conclusion that it is not necessary to have that meeting; but if the cause of liberty requires it, we will all go there, peaceably and unarmed, and we shall return with an increased determination that Ireland shall be a nation." From the corporate cities and towns came large deputations to congratulate the liberated "conspirators," and throughout the provinces bonfires burned on every hill, and newspapers were in great demand; while the *Nation*, in honor of the event and of the triumph of its principles in the person of its chief editor, appeared the following week printed in green ink.

Had the great agitator died at this time the whole world would have revered his memory and exalted his glory; his name would have been a spell to evoke the spirit of liberty in every land and to point the way to freedom's sacred altar. He, too, would have left his people, as he fondly believed they then were, on the threshold of legislative independence, and would have been saved the torture of beholding the gathering clouds of famine, pestilence, and woe which, though yet unnoticed, were fast enshrouding the land in a pall of gloom and untold misery. But such was not his destiny. His soul had to be purified by the sight of human sufferings he could not alleviate, and his death was to take place among a strange people, far from the land and the nation whose applause he perhaps sometimes loved more than a Christian statesman should have done.

CHAPTER V.

State of the country—Its prosperity, resources, and revenue—Diminution of crime—Rev. Theobald Mathew—His birth, education, and services—His political views—Effect of his labors on the national cause—Affection for the "Young Irelanders"—O'Connell's and O'Brien's eulogies on his character.

BEFORE we proceed to trace the current of disastrous events which led to the destruction of the plans and hopes of the national party, and gave to exile or the grave nearly a moiety of the population, we may be pardoned for dwelling a few moments on the social and industrial condition of the country immediately previous and subsequent to the imprisonment of the leaders in the Repeal movement.

The population, the true wealth of a nation, which in 1841, had been officially reported as considerably over eight millions, could have been little less than nine millions in 1844-5, according to the ratio of increase during the previous decades. This addition was principally observable among the agricultural classes: small farmers, cottiers, and tillers of the soil; for, though the masses were never so prosperous, nor better able to purchase the products of manufacturers and skilled labor, the commerce and trade of Ireland were slowly but steadily dying out. The country had, however, been blessed with a succession of rich harvests, and notwithstanding that a large portion of the receipts of the sales, calculated at from twenty-five millions to forty millions of dollars, were annually sent to England to fill the purses of absentee landlords, there was comparatively very little want or destitution. About eighty millions of dollars' worth of farm produce was each year sent across the Channel to feed the operatives of England and Scotland; still, the surplus, at home, was sufficient to supply the necessities of the entire population. True, the food of two-thirds of the people was scant indeed, and their raiment coarse and homespun, but they were content—at least for the present

—living as they did in the fond hopes of speedy political amelioration.

Crimes of all descriptions decreased in inverse ratio to the augmentation of the population. In 1841, the number committed was 9,287; in 1842, 9,875; in 1843, 8.620; in 1844, 8,042; and in 1845, 7.101; or twenty-seven per cent. decrease in four years. The number of capital offences perpetrated show seven a more astonishing falling off. In 1841, there were sentenced to death 40 persons; in 1842, 25; in 1843, 16; in 1844, 20; and in 1845, but 13; or about sixty-eight per cent. decrease in the same period. Of transportable infractions of the law there were, in 1841, 643 cases; in 1842, 667; in 1843, 482; in 1844, 526; and in 1845, but 428; a diminution equal to thirty-six per cent. in four years. Perhaps no country in Christendom can show at any period of her existence such a record as this. Certainly not in these days of modern progress and religious decadence, when even our own newspapers are constantly filled with relations of crimes of every dye and degree without exciting much comment and less public reprobation.

Much of this gratifying improvement was due to the higher tone and more elevating sentiments of national dignity, constantly and persistently inculcated by the writers of the *Nation*, not only in that journal, but in their other literary productions, lectures, and speeches, as well as the example of the Repeal reading-rooms, mainly established and fostered by them. More credit however in this instance is to be awarded to O'Connell, who was perpetually ringing in the ears of his confiding countrymen the great political dogma, "who commits a crime gives strength to the enemy"; and to the Catholic clergy, who were never tired of denouncing secret agrarian societies—the fruitful source of many outrages—and of warning their congregations against all attacks on life or property, as not only against religion and morality but as unworthy of men aspiring to be free.

But the good genius of the nation at this time was a humble Capuchin friar, a man who had spent twenty years of his life as an obscure and laborious priest in the city of Cork, and whose name was known to but few outside his immediate neighborhood. This was FATHER MATHEW. the apostle of temperance, without whose potent and almost miraculous aid the efforts of the Young Ireland *literati*, the influence of the Liberator, and even the moral suasion of the priesthood, would have been weak indeed. Alluding to the result of Father Mathew's teachings on the masses who composed the monster meetings, his biographer, the late John F. Maguire, very justly remarks:

" Though taking no part whatever in politics, Father Mathew was still proud to know that his influence was felt in the political agitation of the day, and was thoroughly appreciated by O'Connell, for this reason— that enormous multitudes of people, who assembled at the call of the political leader, were held in perfect restraint by the controlling influence of the moral leader; and that many thousands of the full-grown population of Ireland met together, in various places and at different times, in all seasons and under all circumstances, and that no instance of outrage or riot ever justified the interference of the watchful and jealous authorities. Large bodies of men, young and old, came from long distances to the places of meeting, and returned to their homes and occupations with a peaceableness and good order that were among the most striking features of that wondrous political agitation, which seemed to rouse the whole manhood of at least three provinces of the kingdom. If O'Connell were able to keep in check an excitable and ardent people, whom he had inflamed to the highest point, by visions of future prosperity and happiness, of glory and grandeur to their country, as the result of that legislative independence which he assured them, and which he no doubt at the time believed, they could obtain—it was through the aid of Father Mathew that he did so; for though O'Connell might have successfully imposed total abstinence from all kinds of intoxicating drink upon his countrymen for a week, or for a month, as was done during the Clare election, on which Catholic Emancipation mainly turned, it would have been impossible for him to have imposed it upon them for any considerable time. And had he to deal with a people liable to drunkenness and therefore ripe for disorder and tumult, he never could have guided his followers for so many years within the narrow paths of obedience to the law, respect for the sacredness of property, and undeviating adherence to the doctrine of 'moral force.' It was to Father Mathew that O'Connell was mainly indebted for the peace and good order which so singularly marked those great gatherings, that inspired the apprehension of the government of the day, and the wonder of those who regarded them with the interest or the curiosity of strangers. Independently, then, of the good which temperance conferred on the people in their individual capacity, and of the greater industry and higher morality which it promoted, O'Connell cherished it as a means to his own ends—the accomplishment of the object which required a thoroughly obedient and docile people to lead. And only in a country elevated and purified by Father Mathew's preaching, could the political tribune have found that thoroughly obedient and docile people."

This extraordinary self-denial on the part of the people was an argument stronger than any other that could have been advanced in favor of their right and ability to govern themselves. When we consider that the Irish are eminently a social and proverbially a hospitable race, we can well appreciate the sacrifices they made at this epoch in order that their grand uprising should not be stained by any act that might lessen its dignity and significance. Besides, it must be remembered that to them the "world was not their friend, nor the world's law;" at least English law, and that any breach of it, when not necessarily involving an infraction of the moral code, has ever been considered, and with good reason, not only not blamable, but, in many instances, highly meritorious. Law, so-called in Ireland, is not made by or for the Irish people; it is not their protector, but the insidious enemy, and instead of being their sword and buckler against wrong and evil-doers, it is simply and absolutely an engine of oppression, a badge of servitude, and a token of national humiliation. Still the people obeyed it, not from any respect for the alien authority which framed it, nor even from fear of consequences, but from the fixed hope that the day was not far distant when in their own legislature they could enact statutes embodying equal justice and equity for all.

O'Connell and his companions counselled this moderation and love of order, as much from political motives as from anything else; Father Mathew, who was not mixed up in politics, but who as we have seen was a most efficient ally of the Repealers, took higher moral grounds. He was a most singular man, and the conversion of his countrymen to the cause of temperance will long remain a chapter in history to astonish and encourage other zealous reformers. "Actuated by motives as inspiring," said Cardinal Wiseman in his consecration sermon at St. Andrew's, Dublin, "a humble son of St. Francis has travelled your land, preaching against a vice which was the greatest bane of your domestic happiness and spiritual welfare; calling upon you to take up the cross of the Church and place it in your hearts, and not on your garments. How has this mission succeeded, and how was that call obeyed? It has been obeyed beyond all human calculation; and the adhesion, not of thousands, but of millions, has proved the *authority* that sanctioned it. Has God not thus extended His blessing even to the most despised among you?"

This is but one instance of the many eulogiums bestowed on the great temperance leader by the highest in position and the most distinguished in morals, in both hemispheres. Born in Thomastown on the

10th of October, 1790, he was old enough to recollect the disastrous issue of the rebellion of '98, and the disgraceful scenes which occurred in Ross, where the gallant Wexford men threw away the fruits of victory, and, perhaps, at the same time the freedom of their country, by the indulgence of their passion for drink. Of an old and respectable family, his early training at school was as good as the times permitted to the children of the persecuted; at home his moral tuition was such as an intelligent father and a loving mother would wish for their offspring. When about seventeen years of age he was sent to Maynooth College, but he did not remain there long, having little appreciation of the discipline then prevailing in that institution. In 1814, having joined the Capuchins, the most humble and least influential order in the country, and after studying under the Very Rev. C. Corcoran, he was ordained, and assigned to the Kilkenny mission; but was soon after transferred to Cork. Here he labored for many years with all his might, among the very lowest class of that "sweet city," the very outcasts of society, male and female, and the good results of his toil were in proportion to his remarkable zeal and perseverance. Few ecclesiastics of our time performed so many distinct duties and with so much good effect as did this lowly friar, whose life seems to have been spent on a determined plan, and to whom every moment brought some task to be executed, some special work to be carried out.

When, therefore, he espoused the temperance cause in April, 1838, he was but adding another labor to the measure of his duties already full; but it was a work of such magnitude and comprehensiveness that it gradually absorbed all others, except those specially pertaining to his sacred office. Strange to say, his first co-laborers were an Episcopal clergyman, a Unitarian, and a Quaker, a strong evidence, if any were wanted, of the cosmopolitan character of his new mission.

The first five or six years of his labors were devoted to root out the vice of intemperance in his native country, and how great was his success, many yet living can joyfully attest. For every year of that period he could average a million converts to teetotalism, and as a consequence the character of the country rose so high as to become the admiration of all, and the special theme of praise with European and American statesmen and moralists.

Though warmly attached to his native land he did not meddle directly with the repeal movement, lest by so doing he might give a political or partisan complexion to an undertaking which was designed to benefit all classes, creeds, and parties alike. He admired O'Connell, fully appreciated his genius, and was glad when he joined the temperance ranks, but when that indefatigable leader, as Lord Mayor of Dublin, somewhat ostentatiously proposed to join the great procession at Cork in 1842, he met with little encouragement from him. "If Father Mathew could," says Maguire, himself a repealer, "by any possibility, or on any pretence, have adjourned the procession, or got rid of it altogether, he certainly would have done so; but Easter Monday was the day specially devoted to such demonstrations, and the temperance societies, throughout an extensive district of the country, had already made their preparations for taking part in it. There was no help for it now, and therefore the best thing that could be done was to put a good face on the matter; which he accordingly did."

For the "Young Ireland" party, as they then were, and for several years after up to the beginning of 1848, he had sincere esteem, and for many of the individual members a lasting, warm, and paternal affection. He admired their ardor, honesty, and nobleness of purpose; he was fond of reading and quoting their soul-stirring poesy and brilliant speeches, and, until the horrors of the famine and the glare of the French revolution of February '48 had driven many of the leaders to premature attempts at revolt, he was in full sympathy with their aims and policy. Even after their failure, and when some were in the penal settlements of Australia, and others in exile in this country, he was wont to speak of them in terms of the highest regard, and to mourn over the infatuation which seduced them from the path of duty into the hazy wilderness of revolution.

In the *Nation* and its able corps of writers he recognized most valuable auxiliaries, not only from their elevated tone and wide popularity, but because they were, with few exceptions, practical believers in his teachings. He in turn reacted upon them, for the men he drew away from the allurements of the public house and the "wake" soon discovered the necessity of other and less deleterious amusements, and found them in the reading-rooms or by their own peaceful firesides. Thus, as the temperance cause was advanced, education became more thorough and general, and the number of readers of good national literature correspondingly increased. This was the end for which the *Nations* contributors strove, and while the Apostle of Temperance was spreading the blessings of sobriety, and its attributes, peace, health, and mental clarity, they were supplying the intellectual food which was to nourish and complete his moral revolution. In one thing both thoroughly agreed: that no people ever rose to true greatness, or recovered their freedom, who were unable to control their passions and subordinate their individual caprices to the general good.

While Father Mathew divided the affections and confidence of the Irish with O'Connell, without being either his opponent or his rival, but for all useful purposes his efficient ally, the political leader entertained and expressed for him, on more than one occasion, the most unbounded respect and reverence. A meeting held in Dublin in January, 1843, which was attended by four bishops, some eighty noblemen, members of parliament, etc., afforded O'Connell an ample opportunity of giving vent to those feelings so creditable to both parties. When the resolutions intended for adoption were submitted to him for criticism he censured them as "tame and unworthy of the object." Snatching up a pen, he altered the first resolution by adding to the phrase, which declared Father Mathew "entitled to the nation's gratitude," the words, "beyond all living men." "What! beyond all living men, eh?" exclaimed a by-stander; "is not that too strong?" "Not in the least," said O'Connell emphatically; "it is literally true." At the public meeting, held to present a fitting testimonial to the good friar, he amplified this opinion with his usual power and wealth of words. Among other things he said:

"The name of the Reverend Theobald Mathew is in fact a spell-word. It proclaims in itself the progress of temperance, morality, prudence, and every other social virtue in the land. I have, as I have already said, come here not to make a speech, but to bear my testimony to his indescribable merits. I could not stay away from such an assemblage as this; for though I feel how little importance my attendance here could be, still I owed it to myself to share in the testimony of the mighty moral miracle that has been performed, and to raise my humble voice in the declaration of my sentiments of admiration at his utility as a man and his virtues as a clergyman, by joining in this demonstration of the gratitude of his country toward him . . . . Having said so much, I ought to retire, for I feel this—that it is not in language to describe, and that there is not rapidity in human speech to follow the brilliancy of his career. There can be no wings given to words, to enable them to rise to his moral exaltation. You might as well think of looking the noonday sun in face, without injuring the vision, as to place the merits of Father Mathew in a clearer point of view than they at present exist. No, and if witnesses are wanting of his utility I call on four millions of teetotallers to come forward with their testimony."

On the same occasion O'Brien, though not yet a pronounced nationalist, delivered a dignified and hearty eulogium on the labors of Father Mathew, on behalf of the county he represented in parliament, which he asserted was benefited much more than any other by his teachings. "Whatever it shall be," he said, in alluding to the proposed testimonial, "will be best determined by the committee; but of this he was quite sure, that they could not erect any testimony so acceptable to him, or so glorious in its results, as an inviolate fidelity to the solemn engagement entered into by the great mass of the nation to the good man." Years afterwards, when the illustrious advocate of temperance had closed, amid pain and suffering, his long and most useful life; and when William Smith O'Brien had returned from his convict home in Van Diemen's Land, he took up his pen to express, in part at least, his poignant sorrow for the loss of his great and beneficent friend. He wrote:

"For myself, whether he be or be not canonized as a saint by the Church of Rome, I am disposed, to regard him as an Apostle who was specially deputed on a divine mission by the Almighty, and invested with power almost miraculous. To none of the ordinary operations of human agency can I ascribe the success which attended his efforts to suppress one of the besetting sins of the Irish nation. If I had read in history that such success had attended the labors of an unpretending priest whose chief characteristic was modest simplicity of demeanor, I own that I should have distrusted the narrative as an exaggeration; but we have been all of us witnesses to the fact that myriads simultaneously obeyed his advice, and, at his bidding, abandoned a favorite indulgence."

There is no mistaking the sincerity of this praise nor of its entire truthfulness; and, coming as it does from a gentleman who was ever chary of his applause, a strict, though liberal-minded Protestant, whose love of his kind led him even under the shadow of the scaffold, it may be considered one of the most appropriate epitaphs that ever graced the tomb of saint or philanthropist.

CHAPTER VI.

Symptoms of division in the Repeal Association—Charitable Bequests bill—Federalism advocated by O'Connell—Denounced by the "Nation" and O'Neil Daunt—English Intrigues at Rome—The Papal Rescript—Financial reforms proposed—Formation of the '82 Club.—The Queen's Colleges bill—The Irish hierarchy on education.

From the day of O'Connell's liberation from Richmond bridewell, a change in his policy was observed by many who knew him intimately and whose affection and respect for his person and great services could not blind them to the sad fact that he was no longer the same fiery, indefatigable agitator, the magnetic orator whose voice could call millions around him and sway them as he listed by the magic of his eloquence. Some attributed the transformation to decaying health and advancing age—he only lacked two years of the ordinary term allotted to men—others suspected that the repeal movement had advanced as far as peaceable agitation could go, and that either the legitimate demands of the people should be supported by armed men, as in 1782, or that a backward step, fatal to all revolutions, political and moral, should be taken. The second alternative seemed the better to O'Connell.

In accordance with this view, the great leader, it is said, upon tolerably good authority, proposed in a secret session of the committee that the Association should be dissolved, and another, under a different name and with what was called by some the "illegal features" of the old one stricken out; or, in other words, to eliminate from the Repeal platform every statement of principle that might give offence or alarm to the English government. This, it will be remembered, was a favorite ruse of O'Connell during the emancipation excitement, and was generally successful, but times and circumstances were now greatly changed. Then it was the organizations that were alleged to be unlawful *per se;* but the repeal leaders had not been indicted, tried, and convicted of crime because they belonged to an illegal body, but on account of attending certain meetings and using language which, it was asserted, was "seditious." Besides, such a change of base at so critical a juncture would be a confession of defeat, a victory for the common enemy, and a source of dissatisfaction among the people. Such at least were the views of Mr. O'Brien and the other members of the committee who affiliated with the Young Irelanders. They protested against such a course as false, craven, and fatal. Mr. O'Connell, at length seeing how distasteful the proposed change was to so influential a portion of the committee, abandoned it for the time, though it is not probable that he ever forgot or completely forgave this first act of insubordination to his wishes, which heretofore had been unquestioned.

The next cause of discord among the Nationalists appeared in a quarter from which it was least expected—amongst the Hierarchy. In August, 1844, against the most earnest remonstrances of priests and people was passed the Charitable Bequests act. By the provisions of this statute no charitable bequest made for a Catholic purpose was valid unless devised six months before the death of the testator, and singular enough three bishops were selected to administer this law, and accepted the trust, though the Catholics of the country almost unanimously looked upon the act with aversion as an insult to their clergy, an imputation on their character, and an insidious attempt on the liberties of the entire Catholic body. The Repeal Association opposed the measure on these grounds; the *Nation* denounced it with its usual force and energy, and the prelates themselves in convocation were divided as to the propriety of any of their number acting as commissioners. Of the proceedings of this meeting, the Right Rev. Dr. Cantwell shortly after wrote to O'Connell the following account:

"The resolution did not meet the approval of all the bishops, neither did it convey to any one of the Episcopal commissioners the most distant notion that in accepting the office he did not oppose the views and wishes of many of his Episcopal brethren. When the resolution was moved, there were six of the protesting bishops absent, and a moment was not allowed to pass, after it was seconded, when it was denounced in the strongest manner by two of the bishops present. They solemnly declared before the assembled prelates that in the event of any prelate accepting the odious office, they would never willingly hold any communication with him in his capacity of commissioner."

Then came O'Connell's sudden and inexplicable conversion to Federalism, involving of course the abandonment of the absolute repeal of the Union, and the obliteration of all the promises, vows, and pledges of the previous five years. There was, it seems, a small knot of Federalists in the north, composed of such men as Grey Porter, Ross, Crawford, and Caulfield, acting, it was generally supposed, on the inspiration of the Lord Lieutenant, Heytesbury, who had addressed the Liberator on this subject and found him more pliant than they had hoped. He even went so far as to write from his retirement at Derrynane a public letter contrasting the benefits to be expected from Repeal and from Federalism respectively, and giving his preference to the latter. As his views were very similar to those of the present "Home Rule" movement, we give the following extracts from this peculiar epistle:

"The Simple Repealers are of the opinion that the reconstructed Irish parliament should have precisely the same power and authority which the former Irish parliament had.

"The Federalists, on the contrary, appear to me to require more for the people of Ireland than the Simple Repealers do; for, besides the local parliament in Ireland, having full and perfect authority, the Federalists require that there should be, for questions of imperial concern, colonial, naval, and military, and for foreign alliance and policy, a Congressional or Federal Parliament, in which Ireland should have her fair share and proportion of representatives and power.

"It is but just and right to confess that in this respect the Federalists would give Ireland more weight and importance in imperial concerns than she could acquire by means of the plan of Simple Repealers.

"For my own part, I will own that since I have come to contemplate the specific differences, such as they are, between Simple Repeal and Federalism, I do at present feel a preference for the Federative plan, as tending more to the utility of Ireland and the maintenance of the connection with England, than the plan of Simple Repeal. . . . The Federalists cannot but perceive that there has been upon my part a pause in the agitation for Repeal since the period of our release from unjust imprisonment."

The last two sentences of this document if nothing else, would have excited in the bosom of the Nationalists a strong feeling of dissatisfaction and regret. They did not care to maintain any closer connection with their despoiler, England. They thought it was close enough already, and whether they would encourage any connection at all with her, should a fair opportunity offer for dissolving it altogether, would depend on the good behavior of Great Britain and the demands of true Irish state policy. They had indeed noticed that there had been " a pause in the agitation for repeal," but had kept their sad forebodings to themselves lest they might have been accused of trying to sow seeds of dissension, but now that it had been openly announced, they felt hurt and irritated beyond measure.

"I felt it my duty," says O'Neil Daunt, his most intimate friend and enthusiastic admirer, " to write to O'Connell on the subject of his recent manifesto. I did not keep a copy of my letter, but I recollect its substance. I stated the general dissatisfaction excited by his advocacy of Federalism. I reminded him that I was publicly committed to 'Simple Repeal.' I told him that no man was less disposed than I was to create discord in our ranks by expressing dissent from the movements of the leader, but that for the sake of consistency I was desirous to exonerate myself from any predilection for Federalism. I concluded by announcing my purpose to repeat at our next day's meeting my former profession of faith on the point in dispute; and, at the same time to vindicate him from the unjust imputation of intending to surrender any portion of his claim for Irish constitutional liberty! 'Do not enter into any vindication of me,' wrote O'Connell in reply. 'Leave every misconception afloat until I reach the Association. We are on the eve of knowing whether or not the Federalists will make a public display. If they do not do so within a week I shall again address the people—not to vindicate or excuse, but to boast of the offer I have made and the spirit of conciliation we have evinced.'"

This was weak reasoning for so great a mind, and, while it may have satisfied a few, it alienated tens of thousands of the best men in the land. The pause of surprise and sorrow which followed O'Connell's letter of October 2d, was interrupted by the appearance of one in reply from Charles Gavan Duffy. It was a production worthy of the distinguished editor of the *Nation;* full of profound thought, clear statements, admirably logical in its conclusions, and replete with plain, broad arguments which carried conviction with them even to the most mediocre understanding. It was now the Liberator's turn to be surprised. Heretofore his sway, though consistent and beneficial, had been despotic. His system of politics was thoroughly personal, but now he became perfectly aware of the fact that he was living in a generation far different from that of the pre-Emancipation period, and that he no longer could control the intelligent masses of the nation except by recognizing their right to a voice and an influence in the affairs of their common country. He found that though he might himself prefer to the solid advantages of a repeal of the Union the delusive promises of the Federalists, and be willing to suspend for a time, or for all time, the agitation for a domestic parliament, others would not do so unless well convinced of the wisdom of the change. "Among the great party to whom he appealed," says a former prominent repealer, "not one voice was heard to suggest a practical step in the direction intimated. The project fell, if indeed it were ever seriously entertained, leaving no memory and no regret."

It had, however, a very disastrous effect upon the harmony of the nation's councils. It lessened the good feeling that had hitherto prevailed in the committee, and strengthened the popular belief that O'Connell was never sincere in his promises of repeal. But though we are not inclined to coincide in this view, it cannot be denied that his hasty adherence to Federalism, and the equally sudden abandonment of it, greatly impaired his influence and, in proportion, increased that of the Young Irelanders.

These were some of Peel's intrigues to disrupt the Association, and were so far successful; but more were to follow. The English ministry had been acting as a spy for the Italian governments on their refractory refugee subjects in Malta and elsewhere, and even, by opening their letters while *in transitu*, had obtained valuable information which, with the true breeding of detectives, they were willing to sell for a consideration. Some were disposed of to the King of Naples, and another part was communicated to the court of Rome, the reward in the latter case no doubt, being the expected interference of the Vatican in the repeal movement. A certain recreant English Catholic named Petrie was the secret agent of the government at Rome, and with that mendacity which generally characterizes an Englishman, when speaking on Irish affairs, he presented the grossest fabrications and put forward the basest falsehoods against the Irish priests and hierarchy. Partially misled by the representations of this unscrupulous emissary, as well as from a natural sense of gratitude for English intervention against the enemies of the Papal States, the Sacred College issued a Rescript forbidding the Irish clergy to take a prominent or violent part in the repeal agitation. The receipt of this document at first, and until its real spirit and contents were understood, created much disorder in the national ranks. O'Connell denounced it as "uncanonical." In the Association, O'Neil Daunt, who, in the absence of the leader was supposed to express his views, said:

"Assuming that this rescript is an injunction to the Irish clergy to abstain from Repeal agitation, what does it amount to? It amounts to a call upon a portion of the Queen's Irish subjects to abdicate partially their rights as Irish citizens. Is this, or is it not, a direct interference with their civil rights? If so, will those to whom it is addressed obey it? Just look at the position in which they would be placed by such obedience. All their lives they have been charged by their enemies with holding a divided allegiance. Now here is the test

—here is the touchstone. If they obey the Papal mandate upon a matter purely temporal—then, by their own act, they will confirm the charge of divided allegiance, against which they have been loudly protesting ever since the very outset of the struggle for Emancipation. The criminal inconsistency of the government in making people swear that the Pope hath no temporal power in the queen's dominions, and yet manœuvring to get his Holiness to exercise temporal power against Irish freedom, is obvious to all. But we, the Repealers of Ireland, are the sworn foes of all foreign dictation in Irish domestic affairs. As much theology from Rome as you please, but no politics."

When O'Connell was afterwards asked if he did not think this was going too far, he answered: "Not in the least. Recollect, my good friend, that what Daunt says, we have already solemnly sworn." But though he had publicly pronounced the order uncanonical he was soon forced to admit and apologize for his mistake. The Most Rev. Dr. Crolly addressed him a letter on the 11th of January, 1845, in which he says: "I was surprised and sorry to find that you had ventured to assert that a letter sent to me some time past, from the Propaganda, was not a canonical document."

And lest there should be any doubt about its character the primate appended a copy of the resolution regarding it, passed by the assembled bishops. It was as follows:

"Moved by the Rt. Rev. Dr. Brown of Elphin and seconded by the Rt. Rev. Dr. McNally of Clogher.

"*Resolved*, That the most Reverend Doctor Crolly be requested to reply to the letter received from the Holy Father, stating that the instructions therein contained have been received by the assembled prelates of Ireland with that degree of profound respect, obedience, and veneration that should ever be paid to any document emanating from the Apostolic See, and that they all pledge themselves to carry the spirit thereof into effect."

The English and the anti-Irish press hailed the Rescript as the death-blow of Repeal, and trumpeted forth the above resolution as the dividing wedge between the priesthood and the people—a consummation, from their stand-point, most devoutly to be wished. Not so, however, did the great majority of the patriotic prelates and priests so understand it. "The Cardinal only censures violent and intemperate language," wrote Dr. Cantwell, "in either priests or bishops, whether they address their flocks in their temples, or mix with their fellow-countrymen in banquets or public meetings. We [the prelates] inferred, and I think we were justified in the inference, that conduct and language at all times unbecoming our sacred character, and not our presence on such legitimate occasions, were the object of this salutary caution."

This was also the interpretation placed on it by the Nationalists. In Conciliation Hall, Thomas McNevin, a gifted young Catholic lawyer, went even farther, and his words were received with great applause. " We are informed, " he said, " that there is an English emissary—shall I say spy—at Rome. Is his the discretion which guides the Cardinal Prefect of the Propaganda ? Do not suppose for a moment that I question the supremacy of the Pope in spiritual matters. Surely nothing is farther from my mind; but, sir, I do question his right to dictate to an Irish clergyman the degree of prominence or prudence with which he shall serve his country. I hope I am not irreverent in doing so. I shall continue to hold my opinion until I am authoritatively informed that he has the right—then I shall be silent. But I never heard before—and it will be a singular doctrine in my view of the case— that his Holiness can take cognizance of the political movements of the Irish people, and use his influence to disarrange the powers we bring to bear in favor of our liberty."

"It (the rescript) announces the undoubted truth," said Davis, "that the main duty of a Christian priest is to care for the souls of his flock, and both by precept and example to teach mildness, piety, and peace. It does not denounce a Catholic clergyman from aiding the Repeal movement in all ways becoming a minister of religion. Nowhere in the rescript is the agitation as a system, or Repeal, as a demand, censured; but some reported violence of speech is reproved."

The writers of the *Nation*, and those who generally acted with them, were in perfect accord with McNevin and Davis, as well as with the clergy and the bishops; and most prominent among the latter was to be found the venerable Archbishop McHale of Tuam, who, a few days after the reception of the Cardinal's letter, attended a repeal banquet at Limerick and delivered one of his characteristic speeches, full of fire, eloquence, and denunciation. "A distinguished Catholic priest," says one of O'Connell's biographers, "who frequently visited Rome, informed O'Neil Daunt that the expression of Irish sentiment and purpose at Conciliation Hall produced a powerful and salutary effect at the Vatican." Mr. Petrie's occupation was gone.

The only apparent change produced by the Cardinal Prefect's letter was a more moderate tone on the part of such of the clergy as were naturally impetuous or justly indignant at the perpetual insults heaped on their countrymen by an alien legislature; but the remote effect was deleterious to the national cause, for it served still more to separate the laity from their old friends and guides and to expose them to the absurd and impractical teachings of amateur revolutionists.

While the Association was a unit on the questions of the Bequest act and the Rescript it was far from being so harmonious on other matters affecting its interests; more particularly on finance. Even before the arrest of the repeal leaders and during their imprisonment, low murmurings were heard against the lavish expenditure of the funds in many useless ways, but particularly in paying handsome salaries to persons who performed no equivalent work. Sinecurists, the relatives and friends of certain pretentious repealers, were, it was hinted, eating up the funds supplied for a very different purpose, and, as no official report of the receipts and expenditure had ever been published, it was insinuated that the treasury of the body was in incapable or corrupt hands. Though no one ever thought of implicating O'Connell in these charges, he saw fit to express his indignation at what he called the unwarrantable interference of the minority, and unluckily took part with those who wished their protégés retained in the nominal employment of the committee, or who had good reasons for withholding statements of account. During his temporary absence from the Association several useless persons had been discharged by a vote of the committee, and considerable money saved thereby to the Association, but on his return he took a decided stand against any further removals. He did not care so much, it seems, for the displaced officials, though some of them were his friends, as for the spirit of insubordination which he believed was manifested against his authority and wishes, and this he could not overlook.

As years stole on apace and as, in the natural course of events, his career in this world was fast drawing to a close, it became apparent to his warmest friends that his love of absolute authority was rapidly increasing, and that signs of a disposition to look on every one who honestly differed from him, as his enemy, became every day more evident. Thus when the 'Eighty-two Club was organized in January, 1845, and when some of his friends who presented themselves for admission and were rejected, doubtless for good reasons, he, though its president, finding he could not control all its actions, ceased to take any interest in its deliberations, and even occasionally alluded to it in terms not very complimentary. As many of the most active members of the club were prominent Young Irelanders we find that the breach was thus gradually but surely widening.

But all these disagreements were insignificant in comparison with the dissensions which sprung up after the passage of the Queen's Colleges bill in July, 1845. The ostensible object of the act was the establishment of three secular colleges in Ulster, Connaught, and Munster, to be supported by the government, who claimed complete control over them, in every particular, and to be open to students without regard to creeds or politics; but the real design, beyond all question, was to fling another apple of discord among the priesthood and the people, to excite discussion between the sticklers for mixed education and the advocates of the denominational system. A faint hope, also, was latent in the breast of the ministry that if those colleges proved a success they could in time be so managed that the youth of Ireland, while being perverted in faith and morals by the aid of English books, British professors, and judicious distribution of honors, might be brought to look with indifference, if not with contempt, on their religion and father-land.

When the bill was first introduced and its leading features given to the public, the Irish hierarchy met in synod and drew up the following memorial, which, as there are statements of principles in it as true and as applicable to education in our day as they then were, are well worthy of reproduction. The prelates laid down the following conditions:

"That memorialists are disposed to coöperate on fair and reasonable terms with her majesty's government and the legislature, in establishing a system for the further extension of academic education in Ireland.

"That a fair proportion of the professors and other office-bearers in the new colleges should be members of the Roman Catholic Church, whose moral conduct shall have been properly certified by testimonials of character signed by their respective prelates. And that all the office-bearers in those colleges should be appointed by a board of trustees, of which the Roman Catholic prelates of the provinces in which any of those colleges shall be erected, shall be members.

"That the Roman Catholic pupils could not attend the lectures on history, logic, metaphysics, moral philosophy, geology, or anatomy, without exposing their faith or morals to imminent danger, unless a Roman Catholic professor will be appointed for each of those chairs.

"That if any president, vice-president, professor, or office-bearer, in any of the new colleges, shall be convicted before the board of trustees of attempting to undermine the faith or injure the morals of any student in those institutions, he shall be immediately removed from his office by the same board."

Whether the Irish hierarchy seriously entertained the idea that the prayer of this memorial would be granted we cannot well say; if they did, they were sadly disappointed, for the bill became a law without as much as conceding one iota to their opinions or in fact to the sentiments of any portion of the people it professed to serve. No, the Irish were to be overburdened with favors even against their expressed opposition. The bishops therefore almost unanimously resolved to denounce the colleges, and kept their pledge so faithfully that in despite of the cajolery, threats, and intrigues of several successive ministries who have lavished honors and money on those institutions, their efficiency at present is a matter of very grave doubt to the majority of the people of Ireland.

On this occasion O'Connell was with the bishops, and he was right. At first he seemed to approve of the project of mixed secular colleges, but when he considered the clauses of the bill closely, had read the memorial just quoted, had reflected on how powerful an instrument those institutions might become, in the hands of an unscrupulous government, against faith, morals, and patriotism, his opinions were quickly changed. He commenced with desiring larger facilities for a higher education of the children of the masses, without regard to religious opinions, he then adopted the views of the hierarchy, who did not, in terms, condemn the endowment of mixed schools, under circumstances and guarantees, and ended in rejecting altogether, as immoral and anti-Irish, mixed government colleges in all their details. Alluding to the advocacy of the Act by certain nationalists, a biographer of O'Connell says:

"These opinions did not meet O'Connell's approbation; he drew very opposite conclusions. The founders of the new colleges hated Catholicity much, but Irish nationality more. The bright lamp of patriotism, which had burned for ages in the gloom of the sanctuary, would languish and die in the glaring light of those academic halls, where religion would be sneered at as an antiquated superstition, and honest patriotism as a "prejudice of place"—both of which should be sacrificed by men of sense for a situation in the colonies or an appointment in England. Servility to aristocracy would be substituted for obedience to religion and homage to God. In short, the godless colleges would be the slave-markets of Irish intellect."

O'Connell, as we have seen, abjured the colleges, not as government foundations but for the irreligious and unpatriotic teachings which he anticipated from them; the Young

Irelanders were perfectly satisfied that the English government should pay the expenses but not select the professors, as the tenth clause in the bill authorized them to do, a very illogical and unreasonable expectation when it is remembered that it was an English ministry dealing with an Irish subject. This latter objection was not offered on the grounds of danger to faith and morals, but from a dread of undue official influence.

" The rising generation, of opposite opinions, mingling freely in those academic halls, would cast aside their sectarian sympathies," they fancied, " and melt into a homogeneous mass of ardent nationalism, forgetful of party feeling and fervently attached to Ireland." In other words, they wished to subordinate Christianity itself to " nationalism, " and while grasping at a shadow would be certain to lose the substance; for without fixed principles of morality and justice, the true offspring of religion, all the merely mental cultivation of which man is susceptible and all the abstract devotion he may entertain for his country, are merely snares to the thoughtless, and worse than delusions.

Mr. O'Brien was particularly emphatic in his opposition to that portion of the act which allowed the professors to be appointed by government and not by trustees. In seconding the adoption of a petition against this clause, he said: "I am not disposed to assist the government in making those seminaries, which ought to be seats of learning, the filthy sties of corruption. It is because I believe that such would be their character if this tenth clause were to remain a legislative enactment, that I shall oppose it to the utmost."

For weeks and months before the bill passed, Conciliation Hall rung with noisy debates on the measure, till the word Repeal was almost unheard or unheeded. Both sections were opposed to certain objectionable features of the act, but the "Young Irelanders" continued to support the principal plan itself, while the "Old Irelanders," as they began to be called, condemned it *in toto.* To do the Liberator justice, it must be said that he endeavored as much as possible to avoid a discussion so fraught with dissensions; and it was only in his absence, at Derrynane or in parliament, that the premonitory symptoms of a near approaching rupture could be noticed. His son, John O'Connell, who had always the bitterness of a fanatic, without any of the honesty which frequently palliates, if not redeems, a character so disagreeable, was generally the first to evoke the evil spirit of discord by appeals to the lowest prejudices of his audience. This naturally provoked retort or vindication on the part of those who favored mixed education. Then followed angry words and simulated expression of a desire to avoid disunion, and the weekly meetings of the Association usually adjourned, and left the sting of defeat or disappointment rankling in the bosom of either faction.

The dissolution of the Repeal Association was now only a question of time. Peel and Heytesbury had triumphed, the incoming Whigs sniffed an easy victory when they again got into office, and the cause of Irish independence was put back for one generation at least. For accelerating this catastrophe O'Connell himself was not blameless, nor were the Young Ireland party, whose views, to speak mildly, were not conceived in the spirit of true statesmanship, or advanced always with proper regard to the well-formed opinions of others; but the chief guilt—for guilt it most assuredly was—rested on John O'Connell, Conway, and such parasites of the Liberator, who thought to find favor in his eyes by the exercise of the most vile and uncalled for abuse of those who differed from him, and whom they went so far as to style publicly as the "baffled faction" and the "infidel party," even in his presence.

CHAPTER VII.

Celebration of the first anniversary of the 30th of May, 1844—O'Connell in Thurles—Action of the British parliament respecting absent Irish Members—Michael Doheny—William Smith O'Brien and John O'Connell—Imprisonment of the former—Debate in Conciliation Hall—Address of the '82 Club—More dissensions—Approach of the famine.

DURING all those unseemly bickerings and sad foreboding, the first anniversary of the imprisonment of the leading Repealers, the 30th of May, was not forgotten or neglected. The special committee appointed to make all necessary arrangements, consisting of Sir Coleman O'Loughlin, Thomas Davis, and several men of like calibre and taste, selected the Rotundo as a fitting place to hold the celebration; and determined that a grand levée, to which were to be invited all Repealers of note in the United Kingdom, would be the most appropriate and most popular manner of testifying their detestation of the cruelty and injustice of English law as administered in Ireland, as well as their esteem and affection for its latest distinguished victims. They felt, perhaps, that from the ominous signs of the times this would be, in all probability, the last demonstration of the kind Ireland would ever behold, and their preparations were on a scale of magnitude such as the capital had never beheld in its palmiest days.

Early on the morning of the 30th, the spacious round room of the Rotundo was filled with corporate delegations, bishops, noblemen, members of parliament, representatives of the learned professions, magistrates, artists, poets, orators, and authors; while in the streets leading to the building dense human masses swayed and crowded, content if they could only catch a glimpse of their favorite champions as they passed in or retired. O'Connell, the chief object of attraction, occupied the centre of a raised platform surrounded by his former fellow-prisoners, and right royally saluted the guests as they were presented to him. "His demeanor," says one who was present on the occasion, " while exercising the prerogatives of his position, was such as became a man conscious that he occupied a throne loftier than any ever yet decked by a kingly crown. But when his official functions were discharged, he addressed the impassioned throng in language too tame for the most ordinary occasion." Alas! though a free man, and surrounded by the sunshine of myriads of fond, warm hearts, the shadow of the prison, the consciousness of defeat, nay, the very mark of speedy dissolution was upon him. "The cynosure of all eyes, the observed of all observers," his was, perhaps, the only heavy heart, the only troubled mind, in that august and brilliant assemblage of Irish Nationalists.

After the levée was over there was a meeting held in the Pillar room—John O'Connell, M. P. for Kilkenny, in the chair. O'Brien moved the adoption of the following resolution and pledge, which, on being seconded by Henry Grattan, son of the illustrious statesman of that name, were adopted with great earnestness and enthusiasm:

"Resolved, That in commemorating this first anniversary of the 30th of May, we deem it our duty to record a solemn pledge that corruption shall not seduce, nor deceit cajole, nor intimidation deter us from seeking to obtain for Ireland the blessings of self-government through a national legislature, and we recommend that the following pledge be taken:

"'We, the undersigned, being convinced that good government and wise legislation can be permanently secured to the Irish people only through the instrumentality of an Irish Legislature, do hereby pledge ourselves to our country that we will never desist from seeking the repeal of the Union with England by all peaceable, moral, and constitutional means, until a parliament be restored to Ireland.'

"Dated this 30th day of May, 1845."

This solemn covenant and agreement was there and then signed by all present, including the Irish mayors, various delegations from the provinces, members of parliament, of the '82 club, and thousands of others; and the scene closed amid general rejoicing and mutual congratulations among the Nationalists. How hollow was the entire pageant, how soon the vows so grandiloquently made were to be broken, was known to, or suspected by, but few.

In the latter part of September of the same year, another and the last of the great monster meetings was held at Thurles, at which about one hundred thousand persons were present. There was plenty of enthusiasm displayed on the part of the people, and O'Connell made the principal speech. But how changed from his former inspiriting and defiant tones! He spoke, indeed, of repeal of the Union, of petitions to the queen and to the parliament, of having seventy Repeal members in that body; but the burden of his address was peace, still peace, and for the first time in his life broadly hinted at the possibility of the defeat of his projects. "I do solemnly declare," he said, "that, even though my efforts were not to be crowned by success, I had rather be engaged in this struggle for the welfare and happiness of my native land, than enjoy all of wealth, and resplendence, and magnificence that the treasures of congregated worlds could bestow on me." Times, however, were rapidly changing, and the high-flown language of the once daring Liberator fell flat on the general ear, and left the heart of the nation untouched. The Repeal Association, though occasionally showing spasmodic symptoms of existence, was really dying beyond the power of resuscitation. The people knew and keenly felt that it would soon be a loathsome, untenanted body, a putrid carcass, without a soul: already given over to dissolution and the worms of corruption.

Some months previous to this meeting a step was taken by Conciliation Hall, which, at one time, it was thought, would have led to grave and very complicated questions concerning the power of the imperial parliament in controlling Irish affairs. The committee of the Association passed a resolution, that all members of parliament who were members of their body should be required to absent themselves from the House of Commons, unless when bills of a strictly Irish nature were under consideration. Upon this, Joseph Hume, M. P., gave notice of a motion in the Commons for a call of the House so as to compel all absentees to attend. The question then arose in the Association, whether the House, under the act of Union, had a right to compel Irish members to attend; and, secondly, if the speaker's writ, in case of refusal, would run in Ireland? A sub-committee, consisting of Messrs. Doheny, O'Hea, O'Loughlin, Mullin, and O'Dowd, was appointed to consider and report on the matter. The members of the committee being all familiar with constitutional law, naturally reported in the affirmative, but upon their decision being submitted to O'Connell he dissented from it, and after some consideration drew up a directly contrary one for adoption by the sub-committee. Mr. Doheny, the chairman, objected to the soundness of O'Connell's legal views, and an acrimonious debate ensued, in the course of which some very unworthy insinuations were advanced by the latter against his opponent. Michael Doheny was at this time an ardent Nationalist, an excellent popular speaker, thoroughly honest, and, withal, a good lawyer, but with all the fire of his native county, Tipperary, he resented those charges and maintained his well-digested views with, perhaps, undue warmth and tenacity, even against all odds.

The result was that O'Connell's report was accepted, and at the next meeting of the Association it was adopted with great enthusiasm. It was also agreed in committee that O'Brien and John O'Connell should be instructed to test the question of parliamentary compulsion: O'Brien, by going to London and thus placing himself within the jurisdiction of the house of Commons; and John O'Connell, by remaining in Ireland to await the speaker's writ.

Those two gentlemen being in the English capital in the latter part of June, 1845, received from the chairman of the Committee of Selection a notice to the following effect:

"I am directed by the Committee of Selection to inform you that your name is on the list from which members will be selected to serve on the railway committees which will commence their sittings in the week beginning Monday, the 14th July, during which week it will be necessary for you to be in attendance, for the purpose of serving, if requested, on a railway committee."

To this O'Brien replied:

"I trust that the Committee of Selection will not think I am prompted by any feeling of disrespect toward them, or toward the House of Commons, when I inform them that it is my intention not to serve on any committees, except such as may be appointed with reference to the affairs of Ireland. . . .

"Desiring that none but the representatives of the Irish nation should legislate for Ireland, we have no wish to intermeddle with the affairs of England or Scotland, except in so far as they may be connected with the interests of Ireland, or with the general policy of the empire.

"In obedience to this principle I have abstained from voting on English and Scotch questions of a local nature, and the same motive now induces me to decline attendance on committees on any private bills except such as relate to Ireland."

John O'Connell also wrote a letter, "absolutely declining to attend," and previous to its delivery returned to Ireland to await the result. Matters, however, were allowed to rest for a time, and it was only in the spring of the following year, upon O'Brien's visit to London, that he again was notified to attend by the Committee on Selection. Though he found that in his absence, and without any consultation with the Association, O'Connell, his son, and several other Repeal members, in face of the resolution which they had framed and supported in Conciliation Hall the previous year, were acting on English or Scotch railway committees, his resolution was unshaken. In reply to the circular again requesting his attendance, he wrote:

"I have been called over from Ireland at a period when the deplorable situation of that country requires the presence of all whose duties connect them with it, for the purpose of resisting a measure by which it is proposed to invade the personal freedom and to suspend the constitutional liberties of the Irish people. In offering resistance to that measure, it will be necessary for me to assist in exposing the systematic misgovernment which has produced those results, which furnish a pretext for this renewed attempt to coerce Ireland. The time and facilities at my command being limited, I do not feel myself at liberty to allow my attention to be diverted from subjects of higher import to matters of local concern, which do not affect the interests of my country.

"I must, therefore, respectfully decline to serve on the committees on private bills, except such as relate to

Ireland. I am aware that the House has the power to deprive my constituents of such humble services as I can render them, by imprisoning my person, contrary to law. I have fully considered and am prepared to abide that alternative."

On the 6th of April, 1846, O'Brien received a reply to his letter, stating, in polite terms, that his reasons did not constitute a valid excuse for exemption, but suggested that, if he would consent to serve at some future period, matters might be amicably arranged. O'Brien persisted in his refusal. On the 27th, the House, on motion of Mr. Estcourt, chairman of the Committee of Selection, ordered Mr. O'Brien to attend the Railway Committee on group II. After its passage, that gentleman rose and quietly said " that he had understood the motion put by the Speaker to be merely a request that he would attend ; he was willing, as he before stated, to do so, in discharge of his general duty to his constituents, under protest against any right in the House to enforce his attendance as an Irish member. But, understanding that the motion put and carried was, that he be 'ordered by the House to attend the Committee,' he begged at once, with all respect, to state that it was his intention not to attend the committee on group II." On the following day the House declared him "guilty of contempt," by a vote of one hundred and thirty-three to thirteen, and on the 30th he was arrested by the sergeant-at-arms and put in the "cellar," or prison of the Commons.

During the debate on the motion for commitment for contempt, the conduct of the Repeal members and other Irish representatives was anything but sympathetic or just. Even O'Connell, when challenged to give some legal reason or authority why the House should not act as it was doing, failed to give any definite response, but contented himself with a half-apologetic, half-deprecatory reply, more objectionable to the proud spirit of his resolute countrymen than open attack or condemnation. John O'Connell, who had but lately declared himself "ready to die on the floor of the House," went even farther in his canting way; and Sir T. Wilde, doubtless to please the parasites of O'Connell and to fan the flame of jealousy that was now so apparent, openly asserted his belief that O'Brien was solely influenced by a "morbid love of popularity and notoriety." To this truckling knight, Mr. Fitzgerald answered emphatically, from his own knowledge, "that Mr. O'Brien adopted his present course, not with a view of making himself a martyr, but in order to serve his country. As for popularity, it was impossible to make him more popular than he now was." On the 1st of June, O'Brien wrote a letter to his friend, Mr. Roache, M. P., explaining his position, and concluding in the following terms:

"I do not wish you to reveal to the House what an Irishman thinks of such a mode of proceeding. Suffering from the injustice of the British parliament, I expect nothing from its generosity. I shall make no further appeal to the House. Yesterday I was extremely anxious to have been allowed to speak on my own behalf, before my committal as a culprit. I shall not again condescend to solicit even this trifling favor. In concluding, I beg most anxiously and earnestly to request you to inform the House that I am no party to any motion for my discharge."

The firm stand of O'Brien, and his consequent imprisonment, created an intense feeling in Ireland. The corporation and the citizens of Limerick passed votes of confidence in him, and fully indorsed his conduct, while his constituents of the county declared that they fully approved of his course throughout. Addresses of a similar nature were also sent to him from Waterford, Galway, Newry, Ennis, Athlone, Cork, Kilkenny, Cashel, Tuam, Ballingarry, and several other cities and towns.

O'Brien was now in confinement for daring to serve his country in preference to English and Scotch railway speculators, and his own countrymen thanked him for his resolute stand. He had taken this stand from a conviction that it was the only one that an Irish member ought to assume; as well as in obedience to the behests of the Association. He, of all who scarcely a year before had pledged themselves not to serve in parliament, remained faithful to his word. What, then, was the Association as a whole to do? What words of cheer and encouragement were to penetrate the solitude of his prison, bidding him resist the unjust demands of an alien parliament to the bitter end?

In the committee of the Association a resolution was offered and passed, indorsing O'Brien's conduct and pledging the Association's coöperation in sustaining his course; but Mr. O'Connell declared it illegal in terms and tone. Upon his suggestion, it was modified; but it again met his disapproval, with an intimation, conveyed through Captain Broderick, that it might be better not to pass it in any shape. Mr. Doheny, who had charge of the resolution, refused to accede to this request, and against the wishes, and even threats, of the sycophants of Conciliation Hall, brought it forward at the next meeting and had the satisfaction of finding it, though in a diluted form, unanimously adopted. It read as follows:

"Resolved, That having learned with deep regret, that, by a resolution of the House of Commons, the country has been deprived of the eminent services of Mr. William Smith O'Brien, and that illustrious member of the Association himself committed to prison, we cannot allow this opportunity to pass without conveying to him the assurance of our undiminished confidence in his integrity, patriotism, and personal courage, and our admiration for the high sense of duty and purity of purpose which prompted him to risk his personal liberty in assertion of a principle which he believed to be inherent in the Constitution."

Still there was not that general feeling of hearty approval of O'Brien's actions that the occasion demanded. It was evident to many that some underhand agency was at work among the people to weaken their sympathy for O'Brien, impugn his motives, or underrate his wisdom, while at the same time to discourage any public manifestations of popular approbation. But his warm friends, and the flower of the Nationalists, were not content that O'Brien should be so slighted, or that the common enemy should indulge in unalloyed satisfaction over their supposed victory. The 'Eighty-two Club, of which O'Brien was one of the vice-presidents, resolved to take action on the matter, and at a more than usually full meeting they passed resolutions and adopted an address, the tone and temper of which were unmistakable. Major William Bryan, John Mitchel, Richard O'Gorman, Thomas Francis Meagher, Michael Doheny, John Pigot, and Terence Bellew McManus, the deputation appointed to present the address, immediately proceeded to London. On their arrival they waited on O'Connell, president of the club, and, after showing him the address, requested him to accompany them to present it. This he declined on the ground that O'Brien, on account of his action since the imprisonment, had refused to receive a visit from him. The address, which was presented without the president, read thus:

"To WILLIAM SMITH O'BRIEN, Esqr.:

"RESPECTED VICE-PRESIDENT AND BROTHER—Heartily approving of the course you have taken in refusing to devote to the concerns of another people any of the time which your own constituents and countrymen feel to be of so much value to them, we, your brethren of the '82 Club, take this occasion of recording our increased confidence in and esteem for you, personally and politically, and our determination to sustain and stand by you in asserting the right of Ireland to the undistracted labors of our own representatives in parliament.

"We, sir, like yourself, have long since 'abandoned forever all hope of obtaining wise and beneficial legislation for Ireland from the imperial parliament;' nor would such legislation, even if attainable, satisfy our aspirations. We are confederated together in the '82 Club, upon plain ground, that no body of men ought to have power to make laws binding this kingdom, save the monarch, lords, and commons of Ireland. From that principle we shall never depart, and, with God's help, it shall soon find recognition in a parliament of our own.

"Upon the mode in which the House of Commons has thought fit to exercise the privilege it asserts, in the present instance—upon the personal discourtesy which has marked all the late proceedings in your regard, we shall make but one comment, that every insult to you is felt as an insult to us and to the people of Ireland.

"It would be idle and out of place to offer condolence to you, confined in an English prison for such an offence. We congratulate you that you have made yourself the champion of your country's rights, and submitted to ignominy for a cause which, you and we know, shall one day triumph.

(Signed) "COLEMAN M. O'LOUGHLIN, Vice-President,
"Chairman."

"May 9th, 1846."

O'Brien, who was deeply gratified at the presentation of this spirited address, received the deputation with the greatest warmth and affection. In his written reply, after thanking them for their friendship and good-will, he said:

"In acknowledging your address I shall not dwell upon the many important considerations which are involved in my present contest with the House of Commons. I cannot but think, indeed, that the constitutional questions at issue are of the highest moment—not alone to the Irish people, but also to each member of the legislature, and to every parliamentary elector in the United Kingdom. Upon the present occasion, however, I am content to waive all reference to all collateral issues, and to justify my conduct upon the simple ground upon which it has received your approval—namely, that until a domestic legislature shall be obtained for Ireland, my own country demands my undivided exertions.

"Be assured that those exertions will not be withheld so long as life and liberty remain to me, until Ireland shall again *fiat* the declaration of 1782, 'that no body of men is entitled to make laws to bind the Irish nation, save only the monarch, the lords, and commons of Ireland.'"

Whoever wavered in this trying hour, it was evident that it was not the distinguished prisoner. His lofty spirit scorned alike the threats of the hereditary foes of his race, and the vulgar arts of the demagogue. He was always firm, dignified, and even reserved, except to his most intimate friends. When the House of Commons found that the edict of their Speaker, instead of being a token of disgrace, was in reality the signal for renewed love and esteem of the Irish for their victim, they resolved to liberate him. On the 25th, Mr. Shaw, M. P., moved that he be discharged, remarking that " the authority of the House had been vindicated by his imprisonment for twenty-five days," and adding that, " in justice to Mr. O'Brien, he would say that the motion was made without that gentleman's acquiescence." There being no opposition, the Irish patriot walked out of his dungeon more imperturbable, and, if possible, more firmly opposed to British legislation than ever.

But the faction that had usurped the leadership of the Repeal movement, and even the control of the Liberator himself, was not satisfied with those proceedings. Jealous of the shining abilities of the Young Irelanders, alarmed at their growing popularity and outspoken method of declaring their immutable intention of obtaining the repeal of the Union at all hazards, it sought every opportunity to thwart and oppose them, and even to induce the great leader, now bowed down with years and labors, to countenance, if not personally support, its petty, malignant schemes.

When the 'Eighty-two Club deputation returned to Dublin their conduct was severely commented on in the Committee of the Association by O'Connell and others; and the course of the *Nation*, in sustaining O'Brien and censuring the members who had, unlike him, forgotten their promises and yielded to English intimidation, was made the cause of withdrawing the support of the Association from that newspaper. The *Nation* and the '82 Club occupied the attention of the committee during several sitings; and while bitter personalities passed between both sections, and charges and counter-charges were made that were not destined to be easily overlooked, the paper continued in the same line of policy, Mr. Duffy and his co-editors pursued the even tenor of their way, undismayed by any threats that could be made against them, and with undiminished ardor in the cause of self-government for their country.

In the midst of all these scenes of quarrel and petty spite the year 1845 was passing away; for the people of Ireland, at least, in actual suffering and destitution, with premonitory symptoms of worse evils yet to come. The very land and its products, at least the most valuable portion, because the most used by the people—the potato—seemed to be cursed by the Great Giver, and to wither like the prophet's gourd in a single night. To the betrayal of some of the popular leaders, the lukewarmness of others, and the unworthy conduct of nearly every prominent layman in what was called the Old Ireland ranks, were to be superadded the horrors of famine and the scourge of pestilence. In October, O'Connell gave a warning note from the southwest. "In my own district," he said, "in the neighborhood of Derrynane, up to Saturday last, there was not the least appearance of disease. But though that particular locality is free from the calamity, the local information in general tells us that the disaster is all but universal—that it is now reaching from the potatoes to the turnips." He plainly foresaw the impending visitation, and proposed the remedy. "This is no time," he thundered, "to be bungling at trivial remedies. The absentees ought to be taxed. The government should declare that they would apply to parliament to tax the property of absentees fifty per cent. I don't shrink from being taxed myself as a resident. I think every resident should be taxed ten per cent, and every absentee fifty per cent. By these means abundant funds would be found to keep the people alive. They should send to the Carolinas for rice—they should send to other parts of America for Indian corn and every other kind of grain, and be able to pay for it out of the public money."

Yet, in the face of this warning, the government remained indifferent.

Father Mathew, whose peregrinations through the south afforded him ample occasion to discover the extent of the calamity, about the same time wrote to Mr. Richard Pennefather, under-secretary in Dublin Castle, detailing the terrible destitution prevailing in Cork and the neighboring counties. He was politely thanked for his information, but no action whatever was taken in the matter.

Playfair and Lindsey, an Englishman and a Scotchman who knew nothing at all of Ireland, were appointed commissioners to report on the state of the agricultural districts; and though they were forced to admit that the exclusive food of four millions of people, and the main sustenance of two or three millions more, was in great part destroyed, little notice was taken of the fact. "We can come to no other conclusion," they said, "than that one half of the actual potato crop of Ireland is either destroyed, or remains in a state unfit for the food of man.

We, moreover, feel it our duty to apprise you that we fear this to be a low estimate."

The whole country was now in a state of alarm, all except the representatives of that paternal government which England persists in foisting on Ireland. The corporation of the capital sent petitions to the queen, that amiable creature who is represented as a model of all the virtues, telling her that strong men and feeble women, mothers and their little babes, were dying or about to perish from actual starvation; and entreating her to call an early session of parliament, that some speedy relief might be afforded the sufferers; but their prayers fell on deaf ears. The representative of royalty in the castle, the hoary schemer, Heytesbury, was waited on by a deputation consisting of the Duke of Leinster, the Lord Mayor, O'Connell, and Lord Cloncurry; but that cold-blooded worthy, who had evidently been taking a survey of the field, laying his plans for the complete destruction of the Repeal movement, and who saw in the impending famine a most valuable assistant, received them with scant politeness, turning them away with false promises of government aid, and vague assurances that there was no real cause of apprehension.

Still the absentees continued to draw their rents out of the country at the rate of about forty million dollars per annum; and produce double that amount in value, which the farmers had raised, but dared not consume, was continually being shipped to England: and still the people went on starving.

CHAPTER VIII.

Opening of Parliament—Coercion and Free Trade—O'Connell and O'Brien in London—Defeat of the Tories—The Whigs in office—Conciliation Hall defies them—Thomas Francis Meagher—Repeal abandoned—O'Gorman, Mitchel, and Doheny—O'Connell's strange course—Trial of Charles Gavan Duffy—Peace resolutions—Secession from the Association.

THOUGH famine stalked the land and everywhere the voice of supplication was raised for help, the English ministry were in no particular hurry to summon parliament. Though the corporation of Dublin and of other large cities had earnestly requested the queen to convoke as soon as possible the supposed national legislature, it was late in the following January when it was called together, and then only to disgust and dishearten, not alone the Repealers, but every person who had the least touch of humanity in his composition. The speech from the throne, as far as it related to Ireland, was eminently characteristic of the English law system as applied to Ireland; that is, simply barbarous, cruel, and mendacious. "I have observed," said the royal lady, "with deep regret, the very frequent instances in which the crimes of deliberate assassination have been of late committed in Ireland. It will be your duty to consider whether any measure can be devised, calculated to give increased protection to life, and to bring to justice the perpetrators of so dreadful a crime."

Now this, in plain language, meant simply the adoption of more oppressive measures for the Irish; additional facilities for wholesale evictions; more policemen, bailiffs, and soldiers to harass and terrify the poor starving peasantry. Accordingly, on the first opportunity, a new Coercion bill was introduced. The measures suggested to be taken for the "increased protection of life," referred not to that of the tillers of the soil, but to the landlords and their understrappers. Their lives were precious in the eyes of her majesty's ministers, but as for the people, the "common herd," they were not worthy of consideration. Though the creatures of the government had already registered several hundred deaths from starvation in the latter part of 1845, and the sapient commissions sent to Ireland by government reported at least half of the food upon which millions of human beings were forced to subsist, absolutely destroyed; though the country had, in its granaries or on its way to England, more corn and cattle than would feed twice the number of the population, and the best-informed circles were complacently calculating, within a few thousand or so, how many millions of Irish people must necessarily die for want of food in the course of the current year; the whole matter was looked upon with such preconcerted and cruel indifference that the complaints of the nation were actually treated with quiet, supercilious contempt. It is not food the Irish people want, they said, but powder and ball; not almoners, but policemen. Still, to keep up appearances, they were pleased to make some show of generosity. One hundred thousand pounds worth of Indian corn was purchased by the government, stored in their dock-yards for awhile, and then, when prices rose, offered at the highest market-rates to the starving people who had no money to buy it. Fifty thousand pounds were voted as a loan, to be repaid, by a local cess, to the Commissioners of Public Works, and an equal amount, on similar terms, for the improvement of waste lands; but in order that as little as possible of those funds might be expended for the relief of the sufferers, its distribution was intrusted to the hands of English officials whose salaries and contingent expenses devoured the greater part.

But, beside the Coercion bill, there was another measure introduced, ostensibly for the benefit of Ireland, but actually one of the most deadly blows ever aimed at a nation so circumstanced as she was. This was the repeal of the Corn Laws. The manufactures of England had increased so much during the century, and had absorbed such a preponderance of the labor of the country, that the producers were unable to supply the home demand, and recourse was obliged to be had to foreign countries to make up the deficiency. On those importations the landholders had succeeded in placing a high protective tariff, which it was now proposed, in the name of Ireland, to remove; and to admit all corn, cattle, etc., into British and Irish ports free of duty. Had Ireland been situated as was England, this would have been a substantial boon, but unfortunately she had practically no manufactures, and depended almost exclusively on her agricultural productions. Whatever, therefore, would bring her into competition with such vast grain-producing countries as Russia and North America, and cheapen food, though a blessing to the operatives of Manchester and Birmingham, would be a curse to the Irish farmers. "With respect to the proposal before us," said O'Brien in Conciliation Hall, alluding to the proposed repeal of the duties on corn, "I have to remark that it professes to abrogate all protection. It is, in my opinion, a proposal manifestly framed with a view to English rather than Irish interests. About two-thirds of the population of England (that, I believe, is the proportion) are dependent on manufactures and commerce, directly or indirectly. In this country about nine-tenths of the population are dependent on agriculture, directly or indirectly. It is clearly the object of the English minister to obtain the agricultural produce which the people of this country send to England, at the lowest possible price—that is to say, to give as little as possible of English manufactures and of foreign commodities in return for the agricultural produce of Ireland."

O'Connell, O'Brien, and other Irish members were in London in March, for the purpose of opposing the Coercion bill, and of endeavoring to extort from the ministry some adequate measure of relief for their suffering countrymen. They did not go to beg or solicit charity, but to demand that a portion of the public money which Ireland had been, year after year, pouring into the imperial treasury, be now used to save the country from wholesale destruction. On this point they were all agreed, and their instructions were plain and intelligible. O'Connell, in a speech delivered by him in Conciliation Hall on December 8, 1845, while advocating the restoration of the Irish parliament, had thus foreshadowed the duty of the government:

"If we had a domestic parliament, would not the ports be thrown open—would not the abundant crops with which heaven has blessed her be kept for the people of Ireland—and would not the Irish parliament be more active than even the Belgian parliament, to provide for the people food and employment? The blessings that would result from Repeal—the necessity for Repeal—the impossibility of the country enduring the want of Repeal—the utter hopelessness of any other remedy—all those things powerfully urge you to join with me, and hurrah for Repeal."

The committee of the Association, in their address, also laid down the true course of the Irish representatives, by saying:

"Your committee beg distinctly to disclaim any participation in appeals to the bounty of England or Englishmen. They demand, as a right, that a portion of the revenue which Ireland contributes to the state, may be rendered available for the mitigation of a great public calamity."

O'Brien had already expressed his views

on the subject in a speech before the Association. "I congratulate you," he said, "that the universal sentiment hitherto exhibited upon this subject has been that we will accept no English charity. The resources of this country are still abundantly adequate to maintain our population, and, until those resources have been utterly exhausted, I hope there is no man in Ireland who will so degrade himself as to ask the aid of a subscription."

With these sentiments the Repeal members took their seats in the imperial parliament: O'Connell's efforts were mainly directed to the defeat of the Coercion bill. In the course of a speech, the last of any importance which he delivered in the House of Commons, he is reported to have said:

"He did not deny the existence of crime in certain parts of Ireland; but he disputed the efficiency of the ministerial remedy. He called upon the government to look into the real condition of the people of Ireland, and to pass the only coercion act that was required— an act to coerce the landlord who would not do his duty. The government had the power in their hands, and if they would take a manly tone with respect to Ireland, they might wave the wand that would turn her misery and poverty into prosperity and happiness. He could trace the outrages which served as a pretext for the present measure to the nature of the land tenure and the anomalous relations between landlord and tenant. The acts passed since the Union showed the many unjust advantages conferred upon the landlord, and the consequent helplessness of the tenant. These advantages had proved the fertile sources of murder—especially that which related to the power to distrain growing crops. There is a season in Ireland—what is called a starving season—for about six weeks before the new harvest; and if the growing crops are distrained, the laborers are deprived of their means of subsistence, they are prevented from digging, and if their wives and children come out in the evening to take a few potatoes, they are consigned to a jail; the husbands of the prisoners are driven to madness; and can it be a matter of surprise that this state of things is a fruitful source of crime—of crime which did not exist before the Union, but which is traceable directly to the legislation of this house? The evils which have been fostered under the existing system are not to be cured by a coercion bill. Similar experiments have been tried several times, and every one of them has failed."

He then proposed as the proper remedy the modification of the Ejectment act, of the grand-jury laws, increased representation, tenant right, and the distribution or abolition of the Church temporalities; and concluded by moving, as an amendment to the ministerial bill, the following: "That, instead of an unconstitutional coercion bill, measures should be adopted by the House to eradicate the causes which produce crime." The amendment, of course, was rejected.

O'Brien, ever anxious about his stricken countrymen, lost no time, on his arrival in London, to ask the ministry what steps had been taken to mitigate, even in part, their destitution. Sir James Graham, in answer, stated, that "instructions had been given on the responsibility of the Government, to meet every emergency. It would not be expedient for me to detail those instructions," he continued; "but I may state, generally, there is no portion of this distress, however wide-spread or lamentable, on which the government have not endeavored, on their own responsibility, to take the best precautions, and to give the best directions, of which circumstances could admit." O'Brien, who had just left Ireland,

and had during the winter ample opportunity of learning the wide extent of the destitution which prevailed in the south and west, and of witnessing the supine indifference of the English authorities in his county, was not at all satisfied with the apparent truth or candor of Graham's remarks. "He was bound to say," he replied, "with regard to the sums of money mentioned by the right honorable baronet as having been on a former occasion voted by the House for the relief of Ireland, that, as far as his (O'Brien's) own information went, not one single guinea had ever been expended from those sources. He was also bound to tell the right honorable baronet that one hundred thousand of his fellow-creatures in Ireland were famishing. Under such circumstances, did it not become the House to consider the way in which they could deal with the crisis? He would tell them frankly—and it was a feeling participated in by the majority of Irishmen—that he was not disposed to appeal to their generosity in the matter.

They had taken, and they had tied, the purse-strings of the Irish purse."

O'Brien's words of warning were unheeded. No relief other than the paltry sum before mentioned was voted at this session, the Corn Laws were repealed, but the Coercion bill was defeated by a coalition of Whigs, Repealers, a few radicals, and some disgusted protectionists, on the 25th of June; and on the 6th of July the Whigs, under the leadership of Lord John Russell, went into office. We shall see farther on how unfortunate for Ireland this change of ministry proved.

The Irish nationalists, though they regarded the Tories as bitter, implacable foes, looked upon the Whigs as even more dangerous, from their seeming friendship, but concealed hatred, for everything Irish. The general opinion that they were about to come into power, and that O'Connell was already in correspondence with them, aroused the indignation of the Young Irelanders. At the meeting of the Association held on the 15th of June, some leading speakers among that party took strong grounds against an alliance with the Whigs, who, it was anticipated, were soon to succeed the Peel ministry; and with whom, it was more than suspected, some of the prominent Repealers in London had entered into treaty for the abandonment of the Repeal movement. Amongst the most eloquent and captivating of the young orators on this occasion was one who was destined to occupy a very important place, not only in the history of his own land, but in this republic—Thomas Francis Meagher.

He was then only in his twenty-third year, having been born in the city of Waterford, August 13th, 1823. All the care that a fond and wealthy parent could bestow on a beloved son was lavished on his education. At the age of eleven he was placed at Clongowes-Wood College, and subsequently tranferred to Stonyhurst in Lancashire, England, where, under the tutelage of the Jesuit Fathers, he grew to manhood, a ripe scholar, an accomplished gentleman, and a patriot whose devotion to Ireland and intense pride in her history, literature, and art, were unsurpassed even by any of the chivalrous and brilliant spirits of that glorious epoch. He was originally intended for the legal profession, but the necessities of the hour, the earnestness of the struggle for national independence, so absorbed all other considerations, that he threw himself into the contest with all the might of his young, ardent heart, and suddenly became one of the most persuasive and forcible orators in the Repeal ranks. His otherwise unoccupied moments were devoted to voluntary contributions to the *Nation*, but it was from the rostrum that he could best move the popular heart, and from whence his words of hope, cheer, and stern resolve, flowing brightly and rapidly, produced the deepest impression and awoke most potently the depths of Irish feeling.

He had already made some harangues in Conciliation Hall, which had equally surprised and delighted his auditors, but on the occasion alluded to he more than surpassed himself. Speaking of the rumored compromise with Lord John Russell, he said:

"Sir: I state this boldly, for the suspicion is abroad that the national cause will be sacrificed to the Whigs, and that the people, who are now striding on to freedom, will be purchased back into factious vassalage. The Whigs themselves calculate upon your apostasy—the Conservatives predict it. They cannot believe that you are in earnest—at least, it seems difficult to convince them of your truth. On the hustings you will dispel their incredulity, read them an honest lesson, and vindicate your characters. On their return to power, the Whigs shall find that, in their absence, you have become a reformed people—that you have abjured the errors of faction, and have been instructed in the truths of patriotism. They shall find, I trust, that a new era has here commenced—that you have been roused to a sense of your inherent power, and, with the conviction that you possess an ability equal to the sustainment of a high position, you have vowed never more to act the sepoy for English faction.

. . . .

"Society—the perfumed society of your squares !—was happy in those days, and loved the amiable Whig government, and would, no doubt, in gratitude for the viceregal balls at which it flounced and whirled, vote for Whig candidates to-morrow. But, sir, the society that is not exempt from the primeval curse—the society that wears out strong sinews to earn the privilege of bread—the society that knows no day of rest, no day of joy, but God's own holiday—that on which he bids the toiler go forth and soothe his sorrows amid the glories of his creation—that day on which many a worn hand may wreathe a garland of flowers, that has been wearing a crown of thorns the livelong week—the society that decks out fashion, that rears up the mansions of the rich, and by which alone, if there was danger on the coast to-morrow, this land could be furnished with a guard for her defence—this, the elder, the stronger, the nobler society has no such memories, no such incentives to subserviency. Roused from the slumber, into which the insidious eloquence of English liberalism has lulled them, the people have started up, and now, for the first time, see before them a country of which they had not dreamt, and a new destiny revealing itself to them, like the sun from behind their old hills, and that destiny expanding into glory as it mounts the heaven and settles high above the island! No, sir, the people of Ireland can never more be duped into subserviency by assurances of sympathy and promises of redress. We have become incredulous of every party in the senate and the state. We distrust, we repudiate, we reprobate them."

No wonder that such burning words found a sympathetic echo in the hearts of his hearers, and that cheer after cheer greeted every sentence, till Conciliation Hall rung again with applause. The young Irish tribune was followed by Mitchel, O'Gorman, and others, in a like strain of condemnation of Whig treachery and unfaithfulness, to which the audience responded with equal vehemence. They believed that the Whigs were even greater enemies of Ireland than the Tories, and they had not long to wait to find their opinions more than confirmed. The views of the Young Irelanders thus presented in the capital, were immediately spread far and near on the wings of the press, and even before Russell and his party were installed in their offices, the people were apprised of their new danger, and firmly resolved to face it manfully.

But, unfortunately, this did not suit O'Connell. He had, during the combined opposition against the Coercion bill, been brought into contact with the Whigs, and, seduced by their plausible promises, had actually consented to abandon, for the time at least, any active agitation for Repeal. When the news of the anti-Whig demonstration in Dublin reached him in London, he forthwith addressed a letter to the committee, which was read at the next meeting of the Association, expressing the " bitterest regret at the efforts being made by some of their juvenile members to create dissensions in the Association." This was strange language for one who, in the heyday of his power, had called the very party whom it was now criminal to denounce, "base, brutal, and bloody." Let us see what their leader, Russell, himself said in parliament about those "juvenile members"—the best blood in Ireland—on the very day they were exposing his mendacity and trickery in Conciliation Hall:

" There is a numerous body in Ireland," he observed, " numerous even among her representatives, which says that no legislation of a united parliament can devise fit remedies for Irish grievances, and that it is in a domestic parliament alone that fit and wise legislation can be looked for. There are others, I fear, who, if I read rightly their sentiments as expressed in a newspaper—I will name it—called the *Nation*, which has great circulation in Ireland—who go beyond the question of the legislative union—who would wish, not merely to have such a parliament as that which it was the boast of Grattan to found, and which legislated under the sceptre of the same sovereign as the parliament of Great Britain, but a party which exerts every species of violence, which looks to disturbance as its means, and regards separation from England as its end."

O'Connell, with a simplicity that could be accounted for only by declining years and health, actually gave credence to this most absurd and utterly untrue statement against the *Nation*. Some time after, alluding to Russell, he said: "He was not the man to put anything forward to serve a party purpose, and was it not time for him (O'Connell) to take up the subject when he found his lordship saying that the *Nation* had a tendency to separation?" There was a time, and that not very remote, when the opinion of his lordship, or of all their lordships in the British Empire, would not have weighed a feather against the truth, honesty, and manliness of the men who wrote for that journal, once his best friends and always his warmest admirers.

But the *Nation*, with its school of writers and orators, had too long been a thorn in the side of all English parties, and much too thoroughly national in its aims and policy, not to be dreaded by the time-servers and place-hunters who now had O'Connell in their keeping. It was therefore determined to get rid of it at once and forever. An unholy alliance of Whigs and so-called Repealers was formed to crush it, and would undoubtedly have succeeded, had it possessed less courage and vitality. The time for the attack was well chosen, but the success of the assailants was only partially assured.

Late in 1845, an article appeared in the *Nation*, in answer to some statements in the English papers, that the railroad system was now so complete in Ireland that, in case of insurrection, troops could be sent in six hours to any part of the country. To this it was replied that in one night all those roads could be destroyed, with some allusions to Hofer in the Tyrol, and other fanciful suggestions as to amateur warfare. This was considered seditious. Duffy was immediately arrested, indicted, and, on the 17th of June, 1846, tried in the Queen's Bench. Every exertion was made to convict him, but the jury disagreed and he was discharged.

However, some admissions made during the trial, that the tone of the *Nation* three years previously was such as might have led some persons to look for entire separation from England as the only true remedy for Irish discontent, was made use of by the clique that passed by the name of "Old Irelanders;" and they, resolving to commence where the government had left off, agreed to bring the *Nation* into disrepute among the people, by misrepresenting its motives and falsifying its statements.

That this was but part of a plan re-arranged between O'Connell and Lord Russell, to drive the Young Irelanders out of the Repeal organization, and to paralyze, if not destroy, the Repeal movement, there can be little doubt, the other portion being the introduction of peace resolutions, which, it was easily anticipated, the ardent and aspiring minds of the young patriots could never endure. Looking back at that epoch in the history of Ireland, we are lost in amazement at the utter absurdity of such a proposition as that embodied in the peace resolution ever having been submitted, seriously, to men who had even the semblance of manhood or patriotism left. It was admitted, in fact, it was the constant theme of hundreds of speeches, books, newspaper articles, letters, and songs, for many years, that the Irish nation was and had been cruelly, barbarously, inhumanly persecuted by England, that her conquest was effected by the slaughter of countless hecatombs of her sons; that her parliament was wrested from her by fraud and violence, and that her people groaned beneath the weight of an intollerable alien satrapy. And yet, in the face of all this, the down-trodden, despised, and outraged people were asked to pledge themselves, that, in case their moderate and just demands were rejected, or answered by more policemen, soldiers, and coercion acts, they would not seek to obtain their rights by the strong arm; that at no time nor under any circumstance were they justified in shedding one drop of blood to secure their inalienable rights and defend their homes and altars. A people who could consent to this, who could so slavishly place their necks under the heel of the despot, would deserve and should receive the contempt and scorn of mankind. What would the fathers of our Revolution, to whose heroism we are all heirs, have said, if such a doctrine had been preached to them before the battle of Bunker Hill or the surrender of Yorktown?

It may be alleged that Ireland was not then in a condition to enforce her claims by the sword, and such, indeed, was the fact. But wherein lay the necessity of proclaiming that she never would resort to arms under any provocation? For such, in truth, were the letter and spirit of the resolution introduced in Conciliation Hall on the 13th of July, 1846. It was brought forward by O'Connell, "to draw a line of distinction between Old and Young Ireland," as he himself said, and read as follows:

"That, to promote political amelioration, peaceable means alone should be used, *to the exclusion of all others*, save those that are peaceful, legal, and constitutional."

The original resolution, passed when the Association was founded, only pledged the members while in that capacity to "the total disclaimer of an absence of all physical force, violence, or breach of the law." Therefore, the new one, which went beyond all bounds of reason, and implied a wholesale condemnation of every hero, statesman, and nation, whom the world loves to honor and applaud, met with the most unqualified disapproval of every lover of his country that day present in Conciliation Hall. O'Gorman, Meagher, Barry, and Mitchel, while disclaiming any intention to resort to physical force, or to violate the principles of the Association, refused absolutely to subscribe to the new heresy; the latter, in particular, delivering a very able speech on the entire subject, in the course of which he said:

"This is a legally organized and constitutional society, seeking to attain its objects, as all the world knows, by peaceable means and no other. Constitutional agitation is the very basis of it; and nobody who contemplates any other mode of bringing about the independence of the country, has any right to come here or consider himself a fit member of our society. I believe, sir, the national legislative independence of Ireland can be won by these peaceful means, if boldly, honestly, and steadily carried out; and with these convictions I should certainly feel it my duty, if I knew any member who, either in this hall or out of it, either by speaking or writing, should attempt to incite the people to arms or violence as a method of obtaining their liberty while this Association lasts, to report that member to the committee and move his expulsion. It is impossible to insist on this too strongly; and perhaps it is the more necessary at this time to explain the fundamental rules of the Association clearly, as the prime minister of England is reported to have stated in the House of Commons that there exists a party in this country who are looking not merely for national independence, but absolute separation, and who contemplate the employment, not of legal agitation, but of outrage and bloodshed to bring about that result. To refute the calumnies of the

English prime minister, and of all our other enemies, it is well to lay before the public once more the real state of the matter—once more to disavow solemnly all intention of exciting our countrymen to insurrection—once more to declare our conviction that all the political and national rights we seek for can be obtained without shedding a drop of blood, and that we mean so to obtain them. In so far, then, as these resolutions purport to embody the rules and constitution of this body, and in so far as they disclaim on the part of the society all intention of resorting to force of arms, I cordially concur in them. And as for the abstract and universal principle which seems to be contained in them—the principle that no national or political rights ought at any time, or under any circumstances, or by any people, to be sought for with an armed hand—even upon any abstract principle, widely as I dissent from it, I do not hold it necessary to raise any question here. . . . I content myself with saying I do not approve of the principle. I do not abhor, for instance, the Volunteers of 1782, who took up arms to procure a political amelioration, and would have deemed it cheaply purchased by a river of blood. 'Free trade or else ———' was the legend on their cannon, and indicates that they reckoned even commercial reform worth powder and shot. And, sir, I hope that even in these piping times no man will tell us that the Volunteers of '82 were criminals and miscreants. America sought a political amelioration, and won it by somewhat similar means. . . . That was a noble deed. sir; and instead of abhorring those Americans, I envy them. Even if we in this hall passed a unanimous vote of abhorrence against George Washington, I apprehend that all mankind, while the world stands, will proclaim him a hero and a patriot. My father, sir, was a United Irishman. The men of '98 thought liberty worth some blood-letting; and although they failed, it were hard that one of their sons should be thought unworthy to unite in a peaceful struggle for the independence of his country, unless he will proclaim that he abhors the memory of his father."

Such were, in general, the sentiments of those opposed to the resolution; but having been introduced by O'Connell, and supported by a faction whose attachment to the Whigs arose out of that species of gratitude which has been defined as "a lively sense of favors yet to come," it was passed by a large majority. The *Nation*, also, was dissevered from the Association about the same time, and the subscriptions sent to it, through the committee, were either returned or transferred to other and more pliable publications. Had that newspaper consented to forget its grand record and to sustain the peace resolutions, it would have received all the moral and pecuniary assistance from O'Connell and his followers it might require upon its new departure. In fact, a proposition to that effect was personally made to Duffy by O'Connell, which, of course, was firmly and indignantly rejected. It gallantly stood its ground, and, if possible, became more vehement than ever in asserting the rights of the Irish people, though in a few weeks its circulation was curtailed by many thousand copies. O'Connell then returned to London, having, as he supposed, thoroughly crushed the Young Irelanders and their organ; and the alliance with the Whigs was considered consummated.

But he was mistaken; for on the following Monday the Young Irelanders, who he considered had been expelled, reappeared on the platform of the hall, and took part as usual in the proceedings. O'Connell therefore instructed his eldest son John to reopen the debate on the peace resolutions, and, if possible, to force a rupture: the Whigs, his new adherents, would be satisfied with no less a concession. That nothing might be neglected that could add solemnity to the fatal quarrel, the Lord Mayor of Dublin was called upon to preside, and John O'Connell moved the resolutions in a speech of several hours' duration. Mitchel replied with even more ability and closeness of argument than on the former occasion, and Meagher delivered his famous speech on "The Sword," which is now, and long will be, we hope, a favorite piece of declamation with the rising generation. He was interrupted by John O'Connell, who impertinently remarked that "it was the strongest conviction of his soul that it would not be safe for the Association to allow Mr. Meagher to proceed. He had no puzzle whatever in saying that the language of Mr. Meagher was not language that could safely be listened to by the Association—that the sentiments were sentiments directly and diametrically opposed to the sentiments of that Association—and that, therefore, the Association must cease to exist, or Mr. Meagher cease to be a member of it." In answer to this uncalled for decision, O'Brien, with his characteristic dignity and forbearance, said:

"He could not allow the meeting to come to such a conclusion without expressing his opinion that the course of argument adopted by Mr. Meagher was perfectly fair and legitimate. He understood they were invited to come there that day for the purpose of considering deliberately whether any gentleman could continue to be a member of the Association, who entertained the opinion, conscientiously, that there were occasions which justified a nation in resorting to the sword for the vindication of its liberties. Mr. Meagher had distinctly stated that he had joined the Association for the purpose of obtaining Repeal by peaceful and moral means alone. But he does not consider, nor did he (Mr. O'Brien) consider that, when they were invited to a discussion of that description, they were precluded from asserting the opinion, which, after all, was involved in the discussion, and from submitting such reasons, as they felt themselves at liberty to submit to their fellow-countrymen, in vindication of the opinions which had been arraigned."

But John O'Connell had resolved to reap the crop of dissension which he and others had so laboriously sown, and, still insisting that Meagher's words were illegal and dangerous, declared that either he or that gentleman should leave the hall. The audience were divided; the younger and more enthusiastic were with O'Brien and Meagher, the older, more timid, or more venal, with the moral-force advocates. The result was that the "Seceders," as they were styled, with a large portion of the meeting, left Conciliation Hall never to return, and the once great Repeal movement received a blow from which it never recovered.

CHAPTER IX.

O'Brien's account of the secession—Attempts at a reconciliation—The Old Irelanders in favor of place-taking—The Dublin remonstrants—Thomas D'Arcy McGee—Position of the *Nation*—Whig treachery—O'Connell in parliament—Progress of the famine.

O'BRIEN, who had not taken any prominent part in the previous discussion of the 13th of July on the Whig alliance, the *Nation*, or the peace resolutions, was yet considered as in some manner the leader of the secessionists, principally from his high social standing, mature years, large experience of public affairs, and natural gravity of character. In a letter addressed by him to the Rev. Dr. Miley, December, 1846, he thus recounts, in a calm, dispassionate manner, the causes of the division in the Association, so disastrous to Irish hopes and aspirations:

"Negotiations were opened between Mr. O'Connell and the Whigs at Chesham Place. 'Young Ireland' protested, in the strongest terms, against an alliance with the Whigs. Mr. O'Connell took offence at the language used by Mr. Meagher and others. When I arrived in Dublin, after the resignation of Sir Robert Peel, I learned tha the contemplated a rupture with the writers of the *Nation*. Before I went to the county of Clare, I communicated, through Mr. Ray, a special message to Mr. O'Connell, who was then absent from Dublin, to the effect that, though I was most anxious to preserve a neutral position, I could not silently acquiesce in any attempt to expel the *Nation* or its party from the Association. Next came the Dungarvan election, and the new 'moral force' resolutions. I felt it my duty to protest against both at the Kilrush dinner. Upon my returning to Dublin I found a public letter from Mr. O'Connell, formally denouncing the *Nation*, and no alternative was left me but to declare that, if that letter were acted upon, I could not coöperate any longer with the Repeal Association. The celebrated two-day debate then took place. Mr. J. O'Connell opened an attack upon the *Nation* and upon its adherents. Mr. Mitchel and Mr. Meagher defended themselves in language which, it seemed to me, did not transgress the bounds of decorum or of legal safety. Mr. John O'Connell interrupted Mr. Meagher in his speech, and declared that he could not allow him to proceed with the line of argument necessary to sustain the principles which had been arraigned. I protested against this interruption. Mr. J. O'Connell then gave me to understand that, unless Mr. Meagher desisted, he must leave the hall. I could not acquiesce in this attempt to stifle a fair discussion, and sooner than witness the departure of Mr. J. O'Connell from an association founded by his father, I preferred to leave the assembly.

"Soon after this occurrence I intimated to Mr. O'Connell, by a private message, conveyed through his son, my readiness to assist in bringing about an accommodation, in case he felt disposed to change his conduct with respect to the Young Ireland party. He preferred to proceed in a career, of which we have since witnessed the full development. He induced the committee to stop the circulation of the *Nation*. Having failed to ruin the property of Mr. Charles Gavan Duffy (whom I believe to be not only one of the ablest men in this kingdom, but also one of the most virtuous), he next arraigned him as guilty of high-treason by a formal indictment, which was sustained by neither legal nor constitutional argument, but was marked by all the perverted ingenuity of a crafty attorney-general. He has since endeavored by most ungenerous means to fix upon Mr. Duffy, and upon his friends, the charge of infidelity in regard to religious belief."

Such was the forbearance exercised by O'Brien and his associates upon being actually expelled from an association they had helped so much to extend and foster, by their example and unceasing teachings. The country was at first shocked and then stupefied by the loss of so many able and uncompromising advocates. At the beginning, it was hoped that the breach might be closed, and an unsuccessful attempt was even made by a few distinguished clerics and lay gentlemen to heal the wound which the national cause had received, but in vain; the faction who held possession of the hall, its records, and funds, were resolved that they should rule or ruin. Week after week, and day after day, the foulest epithets were applied, from the platform, and through the Whig-Repeal newspapers, to the seceders. They were called blasphemous, infidel, and revolutionary, and the very worst passions of the low Dublin mob were continually excited against them individually and collectively. Even O'Connell so far forgot his ancient dignity and love of fair play as to attempt to hold them up to ridicule. He did more; he sought to undermine the independence and vitiate the opinions of those of any note who continued to take part in the proceedings of the Association, by placing before their eyes, as a reward for their servility and debasement, the hope of government patronage. "There were," he said, at the meeting subsequent to the secession, "a great many young men of talent—Repealers in principle—who were afraid to join the Association lest they should thereby deprive themselves of the chance of obtaining the honors and dignities of their professions. I am happy to be able to say that I have reason to know it is the opinion of Lord Besborough (Whig Lord Lieutenant), that the fact of a man's being a Repealer is no reason at all for excluding him from office." And to make the information more explicit and pointed, he added: "Young Ireland stands up and opposes those who take office under the government, by calling them 'apostates.'"

Pending negotiations between the Young and Old Ireland parties, which were initiated and conducted mainly by the Rev. Dr. Miley, a learned priest, and an Irishman of sincere but moderate views, but which proved to be an utter failure, a number of citizens of Dublin, old members of the Repeal organization, associated themselves together under the title of Remonstrants, for the purpose of assisting the self-imposed task of Dr. Miley, as well as to show the malcontents of Conciliation Hall that the mass of the intelligent men of the capital had no sympathy with the arbitrary course pursued by John O'Connell and his supporters. They were composed principally of shopkeepers and young mechanics—the most respectable of their class in the city—and were headed by Martin Crean, Joseph Hollywood, Halpin, Barry, and others. After a few weeks spent in quietly canvassing the opinions of their fellow-workmen, they drew up a respectful remonstrance against the unwarrantable action of the Old Ireland faction and the expulsion of O'Brien and his friends, and having presented it in form on the 24th of October, it was ordered by John O'Connell not only to be rejected, but to be cast literally into the gutter. The two thousand men who had signed the document felt indignant at this treatment, as did, indeed, the general public, so they resolved to hold a public meeting in the

Rotundo to express their indignation at the insult.

The meeting took place on the 3d of November, and was very largely attended. Some signs of opposition were shown by the mob, composed chiefly of coal-porters, and attempts were made to force in the doors and break up the assembly by sheer violence, but the tradesmen inside quickly dispersed their "moral force" assailants. The principal speaker on that occasion was a young man whose name had been hitherto unknown in Irish politics, THOMAS D'ARCY MCGEE, but who, though only in his twenty-second year, had acquired considerable reputation as a writer and orator at this side of the Atlantic. Mr. McGee was a native of Carlingford, in the county of Louth, where he was born on the 13th of April, 1825, though most of his boyhood was spent in Wexford amid those historic scenes of that county which have long been celebrated in Irish history. When seventeen years old he emigrated to the United States, and, settling in Boston, became connected with the *Pilot*, first, in a subordinate capacity, and, next, as editor. In this latter capacity he had many occasions for studying from a distance and with perfect impartiality the workings of the Repeal Association, and the drift of the younger and more resolute elements in the organization. The *Pilot*, then the only Irish Catholic journal of any note published in the eastern portion of the United States, was, as it still is, one of the most popular and widely circulated of the weekly press; and being frequently quoted abroad on Irish-American subjects, its articles generally attracted much attention in Ireland. After the imprisonment and liberation of O'Connell, its editor, Mr. McGee, was invited by Doctor, now Sir John Gray, of the *Daily Freeman's Journal*, to take a position on his editorial staff. In 1845, Mr. McGee, being naturally anxious to return home, accepted the invitation, and for nearly a year acted as special London correspondent of the *Freeman*. While in the English capital the news reached him of the disruption in Conciliation Hall; and as the

Freeman appeared to take sides with the Old Irelanders, he cancelled his engagement, and, returning to Dublin, became one of the editors of the *Nation*.

The three years he had spent in this country, his indefatigable labors in every part of New England to establish auxiliary Repeal Societies, and his practical acquaintance with the workings of our republican system, as well as his subsequent knowledge of parliamentary affairs acquired as London correspondent, fitted him admirably for the position of spokesman of the Remonstrants; and as he had taken no part whatever in the previous discussions in the Associations, his mind could not be supposed to be warped by any of the personal feeling or local jealousy so apparent in the struggles of the rival Repeal parties. The meeting was a success; and the citizens, recovered from the onslaught made on their rights in the talismanic name of their great chief, began to breathe more freely. The awe, the spell, that still hung round the very name of O'Connell, was dissipated, and it was then and there determined that if the Old Irelanders would not abandon their absurd Quaker doctrines, and more criminal subserviency to the Whigs, a new national organization should be founded to continue the agitation, on the original basis of no compromise with the enemies of the country till the demands of the people for a domestic legislature were conceded.

To carry out this design, all hope of a reconciliation having failed, a second meeting was held on the 2d of December. The Round Room of the Rotundo was at an early hour filled with men and women of the very best classes in society—solid traders, skilled mechanics, enthusiastic students, and professional men of all ages and degrees. The leading seceders were escorted to the hall by platoons of working men, for so rife was the spirit of violence among the mob, instigated thereto by the advocates of moral suasion, that it was feared, and not without reason, that freedom of speech was not only not to be tolerated in Conciliation Hall, but in every part of the metropolis where the rowdies of Burgh Quay held sway. All the leaders of the Young Ireland party then in the city attended, and most of them, as well as the representative of the Remonstrants, addressed the assemblage, and amid the warmest greetings vindicated their past course in calm, firm, and well chosen terms. The previous suggestion for the establishment of a permanent organization was also presented to this meeting, and, on being favorably received, a day was set apart for the formation of a new Repeal Society.

From the expulsion of the Young Irelanders from the Repeal Association, and the virtual condemnation of their organ, the *Nation*, by O'Connell and those who agreed with him, the course of that remarkable newspaper was singularly dignified, candid, and manly. It was even conciliatory, as far as was consistent with the advocacy of its principles, towards its most virulent enemies. It met slanders and falsehoods of the deepest dye with short notice or contemptuous silence; but when anything like argument was adduced against it, it replied in the best of temper, and with a force of logic so overwhelming, that it seldom became necessary to refer a second time to any one charge advanced against it. The hostility of O'Connell and the calumnies of the place-hunters had succeeded in reducing its subscription list, perhaps a hundred per cent at first, but this loss was partly made good by the patronage of a middle class of Irishmen, who, while they loved their country and desired legislative independence for her, could never brook the absolutism and assumption which characterized a few of the leaders of the Association.

Charles Gavan Duffy, who was from its commencement the editor-in-chief, was now also the principal proprietor of the paper; John Mitchel, one of its most forcible and trenchant writers, ranked next in point of seniority, and then followed Thomas Devon Reilly and Thomas D'Arcy McGee, each in his way gifted with peculiar and remarkable talents as a journalist. Of these four, Reilly is the least known; partly from the collapse of the Young Ireland movement, but mainly from his untimely death, which took place in this country several years ago, before he had reached the years of mid-life. He was, nevertheless, an accomplished and facile writer, more solid than brilliant, and less likely to be carried away by poetic imaginings and mere word-painting than many of his contemporaries. He had been a neighbor of Duffy's in his boyhood, and in his maturity he enjoyed for a long time the confidence and esteem of that patient cultivator of young genius, and profound master of the pen.

The contributors to the columns of the *Nation* at that period were legion, and included such names as those of Miss Elgee ("Speranza"), now Lady Wilde; "Eva," Mrs. Dr. Callan; R. D. Williams ("Shamrock"); Denis Florence McCarthy ("Desmond"); James Clarence Mangan ("Terre Filius" and "J. C. M."); Davis ("The Belfast Man"); J. de J. Frazer, Meagher, O'Gorman, Dr. Kane of Kilkenny, Rev. C. P. Meehan, J. B. Dillon, McDermott, Samuel

Ferguson, Pigot, and a host of others, who, in poetry or prose, all aimed at the same object—the elevation of the Irish race from the slough of mental as well as physical bondage, and the regeneration of their country, by teaching its sons how to win and deserve freedom. "To create and to foster a public opinion in Ireland, and to make it racy of the soil," was the motto chosen for the first number of the paper, and never did one publication in the English, or any other language, gather around it, to execute its designs, so much rare ability, genuine merit, and lofty national spirit. Easily flinging from its skirts, as unworthy of serious notice, the filth that was thrown at it by the Castle hirelings in and out of Conciliation Hall, it continued each successive week to pour its broadsides into that corrupt amalgamation of cheats and frauds called the Liberal party, while its appeals to the nationalists, its reports and reviews on Irish industry and literature, its sweet songs and historical ballads, found their way into every Irish household, and rekindled the smouldering fires of patriotism which had wellnigh been extinguished by the cowardice and subserviency of the underlings of the Association.

But there was an enemy in Ireland, and that, too, under the special patronage of the British government, against which the *Nation* and its brilliant phalanx were powerless,—the Famine. Like a terrible pall, it spread over the entire face of the land, carrying destruction, disease, and death to hundreds of thousands of households. The very atmosphere seemed poisoned with its breath; and the healthful saline breezes that blow in on its shores from the west, appeared to be overladen with pestilence the moment they touched the mountains or descended into the valleys. In the midst of plenty, for the grain crop and the dairy produce were never more prosperous than in the autumn of 1846, the people were dying by scores, by hundreds, and by thousands, on their cold hearths, in the bleak fields, and by the roadside.

But it may be said, What did the liberal

Whigs do to alleviate this fearful calamity, to stay this tide of woe and national disaster? They had promised justice to Ireland; and O'Connell, in order to give them another trial, had virtually abandoned his agitation, and had driven from the Repeal ranks all who were manly and uncompromising among his supporters. Did they keep their covenant and arrest the progress of the famine? On the contrary, they encouraged it, helped it along, in fact, and, with an ingenuity truly diabolical, used the very means provided for the relief of the Irish, for the purpose of extirpation or total destruction. Before the crimes of that sleek, smooth-spoken, treacherous English party, the atrocities of the Red Earl, Sydney, Montjoy, and Cromwell, pale their ineffectual fires, and become in Irish history mere trifles either in deliberation of purpose or worse than savageness of execution.

The last appearance of O'Connell in Parliament was in January, 1847. Broken down in health, sickened and disappointed at the awful state of his country, he rose totteringly in his seat, and with feeble, but still pathetic accents implored the imperial legislature to interpose and stay the tide of Irish famine; but in vain. His power was gone, his strength was sped. His locks had been shorn by the Whig Delilah, and he had become a subject of brutal mirth to the modern Philistines. The party for whose friendship he had bartered the love and confidence of so many of his gifted countrymen, and for whom he had turned his back on the glorious history of the past, treated his appeals and demands with equal scorn —till, thoroughly overcome by their base treachery; he vanished from the House of Commons, so long the scene of his contentious victories, and returned no more.

To keep up the illusion of charitableness, however, the party in authority voted fifty thousand pounds to be expended in the most plague-stricken districts, and passed what was called a Labor-Rate act. By this cunning device money was to be raised by the imposition of a new and additional tax on each Poor Law district; but, instead of being expended by the local authorities, it was to be controlled by the government, which means by its officials, most of whom were sent over from England, totally ignorant of the wants of the people, and whose salaries ate up more than half of what was levied on the country. No better plan could have been adopted to increase pauperism and to utterly ruin the small farmers, who, unable to pay the excessive tax, were obliged to abandon their little farms, seek refuge in emigration, or descend to the rank of beggars, and thus increase the mass of destitution and disease that prevailed throughout. "It is enough to say," says Mr. Mitchel, "that in this year, 1846, not less than three hundred thousand perished, either of mere hunger, or of typhus fever caused by hunger."

No powers of description, no imagination, no matter how inventive, no words, nor combination of words, can adequately convey the faintest impression of the unheard-of suffering endured by the Irish people at that time. The most callous mind, the greatest stoic, cannot but turn away from the mere mention of the loathsome effect produced by famine and fever combined. Here is an account of Skibbereen, which might with equal truth have been applied to many other localities, taken from a letter addressed to the Duke of Wellington by N. M. Cummins, Justice of the Peace, in December, 1846.

"I accordingly went, on the 15th, to Skibbereen, and to give the instance of one townland which I visited, as an example of the state of the entire coast district, I shall state simply what I there saw. It is situated on the eastern side of Castlehaven Harbor, and is named South Reen, in the parish of Mycross. Being aware that I should have to witness scenes of frightful hunger, I provided myself with as much bread as five men could carry, and on reaching the spot I was surprised to find the wretched hamlets apparently deserted. I entered some of the hovels to ascertain the cause, and the scenes that presented themselves were such as no tongue or pen can convey the slightest idea of. In the first, six famished and ghastly skeletons, to all appearance dead, were huddled on some filthy straw, their sole covering what seemed a ragged horse-cloth, their wretched legs hanging about, naked above the knees. I approached in horror, and found, by a low moaning, that they were alive—they were in fever: four children, a woman, and what had once been a man. It is impossible to go through the detail; suffice it to say that, in a few minutes, I was surrounded by at least two hundred of such phantoms, such frightful spectres as no words can describe. By far the greater number were delirious, either from famine or from fever. Their demoniac yells are still ringing in my ears, and their horrible images are fixed upon my brain. My heart sickens at the recital, but I must go on.

"In another case decency would forbid what follows, but it must be told. My clothes were nearly torn off in my endeavor to escape from the throng of pestilence around, when my neck-cloth was seized from behind by a grip that compelled me to turn. I found myself grasped by a woman, with an infant, apparently just born, in her arms, and the remains of a filthy sack across her loins—the sole covering of herself and babe. The same morning the police opened a house on the adjoining lands, which was observed shut for many days, and two frozen corpses were found, lying upon the mud floor, half devoured by the rats.

"A mother, herself in fever, was seen the same day to drag out the corpse of her child, a girl about twelve, perfectly naked, and leave it half-covered with stones. In another house within five hundred yards of the cavalry station at Skibbereen, the dispensary doctor found seven wretches lying, unable to move, under the same cloak. One had been dead many hours, but the others were unable to remove either themselves or the corpse."

Such is the horrible picture as sketched

by no less a personage than a high local official of the government—the paternal government of England—whose sympathies for Ireland were so much vaunted by the recreants of Conciliation Hall, and for condemning whom, the "juvenile members" were accused of endeavoring to sow dissension and of provoking disunion.

CHAPTER X.

Attempts at reunion—John B. Dillon—The Irish Confederation—Its organization and aims—The Galway election—More overtures for union—Charles Gavan Duffy—
—Rev. C. P. Meehan.

THE latter half of the year 1846 was spent by the expelled members of the Repeal Association in various ways which they individually considered the most likely to keep alive the spirit of Irish patriotism, and to save it from sinking beneath the triple weight of Whig misgovernment: Repeal, sycophancy, and the famine. Still, the hope of a reorganization of the Association was not altogether abandoned. O'Brien published several letters on the subject, exhibiting great good sense and moderation, and, pending the result of Dr. Miley's negotiation, he recommended the formation of a literary society for the promulgation of thoroughly national opinions and general intelligence on Irish subjects, each member to take up a special topic for his task.

Consistently with his own suggestion, he himself took up that of Land Tenure, and treated it in a very masterly manner.

John B. Dillon, one of the original founders of the *Nation*, but at that time a practising barrister of high repute, also published a letter in the metropolitan press, advocating a reunion of the dissevered elements. Among other reasons adduced by him why this should be effected at once, were the following:

"The position in which the country is now placed presents to the Repeal leaders a noble opportunity of pushing forward the Repeal cause, by giving practical demonstration of the utility of home legislation. The whole people of Ireland are at length united in one sentiment—dissatisfaction with things as they are, and a desire for change. The landlords, in terror for their estates, are compelled, in self-defence, to consider the condition and necessities of the country, and are prepared to enter on any safe and honorable course that leads out of the difficulties which surround them. If the committee of the Association could *now* stand before the country as the instructors of the English government—if it possessed wisdom to originate useful measures, and influence to compel their adoption, the advantages of self-government would be made plain to all, and decency itself would compel our English rulers to abandon duties which they discharged under the guidance of others. This, my dear sir, I take to be the *rationale* of 'moral force.' To seek for change by moral force is not to shout for it, but to demonstrate its utility. And the only way to demonstrate the utility of Repeal is, by showing that we can do our own business better than others can do it for us."

But the Old Irelanders were beyond conviction or the reach of appeals; and to the fair and candid approaches of the nationalists they returned nothing but personal and vulgar abuse, mixed with a sort of sanctimonious cant in which John O'Connell, and such thoroughly debased men as Robert Dillon Browne, Sommers, Reynolds, Costelloe, and others, of neither private nor public character, who now occupied each week the platform of Conciliation Hall, were experts. The inhuman policy of the Whigs, the groans of millions of their starving countrymen could not move them from their schemes of ruin, nor stay their thirst for office. They went headlong to their own, and, unfortunately, to the nation's, destruction.

No other course being left, the seceders resolved to form a new organization and endeavor to revise the sinking cause of national independence. The 13th of January, 1847, was the day chosen for the first meeting; and on that occasion the large room of the Rotundo was crowded to its ultimate capacity by gentlemen and ladies, the intelligent mechanics of the city, and professional men from all parts of the country. About a hundred of the principal movers in the matter occupied the platform, amongst whom were O'Brien, O'Gorman, Sr., O'Gorman, Jr., Captain Bryan, Major Talbot, Lawlor, Duffy, Martin, McGee, Mitchel, O'Hagan, Meagher, Reilly, Taaffe, Dillon, Haughton, Barry, McCarthy, McManus, O'Callaghan, Doheny, Crean, etc. John Shea Lawlor occupied the chair; Duffy and Dillon acting as secretaries.

O'Brien was the first and principal speaker. He dwelt at considerable length and with great emphasis on all the circumstances which had preceded, accompanied, and followed the retirement of himself and friends from Conciliation Hall. Passing to the objects to be attained by the new organization about to be formed, he said:—

"Our object will be to combine every section and class of the Irish people in one united effort to obtain the legislative independence of Ireland. From the hour I joined the Repeal Association to the present moment, I have been of the opinion, and, whenever I have had the opportunity, I have delivered that opinion, that the repeal of the Union could not be carried until there be a much greater union among classes and creeds than there is at present. Repeal cannot be carried by the democracy alone, nor by the aristocracy alone; but it can be carried by the combination of the nobles, gentry, and people of Ireland, and carried without one moment's struggle. Well, then, gentlemen, remember it will be your solemn, your important duty, to prove in every way in your power that your fellow-countrymen may depend on your moderation, on your sense of justice, on your toleration of adverse opinion, whether in politics or religion, that there is no man among you who does not desire to sustain the rights of property, which can be of no value if not equally valuable to you as to the highest and wealthiest member of society. Deprive men of the argument which is now used, that your object is to establish Catholic ascendency. Believe me, the proceedings of the last three months have done much to shake that argument. Is there one single advantage that Catholics could obtain from Repeal, that Protestants should not share? For my part, I am not able to discover such an advantage; and I here declare, what I have declared before at the hustings, in Limerick and elsewhere, that if there were to be an attempt made to establish Catholic ascendency, no man would more vehemently oppose the attempt than I. But, gentlemen, those apprehensions appear to me, and ever did, to be entirely visionary. Still they have existed, and a remnant of them still exists. Be it your most earnest endeavor, each in his individual sphere, to remove those apprehensions."

The speaker concluded his lengthy and lucid address by moving the following resolutions, which, having been seconded by Michael Joseph Barry of Cork, in a very able speech, were passed by acclamation:—

"'That Domestic Legislation is now, as it has been for forty-six years, the great and urgent want, as well as the inalienable right, of the Irish Nation; and that the helpless and dependent condition of Ireland, under the calamity of this present season, has made that necessity more apparent and more imperative.

"'That circumstances having rendered it impossible for us to coöperate, as members, with the existing Association, which was instituted to seek this great national object, it becomes our duty to make ourselves a separate sphere of activity, in which we may humbly strive for our country's independence in the way that seems to us best suited to attain it. But we desire to have it clearly understood that, in taking this step, we disclaim all antagonism to the Association already in existence, to which we wish success in every honest effort it may make in furtherance of Repeal.

"That a society be now formed under the title of 'The Irish Confederation,' for the purpose of protecting our national interests and obtaining the Legislative Independence of Ireland, by the force of opinion, by the combination of all classes of Irishmen, and by the exercise of all the political, social, and moral influence within our reach."

Doheny, Meagher, and several other gentlemen spoke on this occasion; and in allusion to the resolution, "that the basis and essence of 'the Irish Confederation' shall be absolute independence of all English parties; and that any member of the Council, accepting or soliciting for himself or others an office of emolument under any government not pledged to effect the Repeal of the Union, shall thereupon be removed from the Council,"—Meagher said:—

"It gives me sincere delight to move this resolution. I know you will adopt it—I am confident you will act up to it boldly. Public men have said that the cause of

Repeal is strengthened by Repealers taking places. I maintain that it is weakened. The system decimates the ranks. In 1843, where were the Repealers who assumed the official garb—after the movement of 1834?

"Repealers occupying office may not abandon their opinions, but they withdraw their services. It is impossible to serve two masters. You cannot serve the minister who is pledged to maintain the Union, and serve the people who are pledged to repeal it. Will the report on the financial grievances, inflicted by the Union, accompany a treasury minute from London? Will you get a farthing a week, a penny a month, or a shilling a year from the Mint? Will a Repeal pamphlet issue from the Board of Public Works? The Trojans fought the Greeks through the streets of Troy, in Grecian armor. Will the Repealers fight the Whigs upon the hustings, with Whig favors in their pockets? Recollect, the Union was carried by Irishmen receiving English gold. Depend upon it, the same system will not accelerate its repeal. Sir, we must have an end of place-begging. The task we have assumed is a serious one. To accomplish it well, our energies must have full play. The trappings of the Treasury will restrict them more than the shackles of the prison. State liveries usually encumber men, and detain them at the Castle gates. Not a doubt of it, we shall work the freer when we wear no royal harness."

It was under these auspices, and with such solemn pledges, that the Irish Confederation was formed, and new hope gleamed athwart the face of the famine-stricken land even in her gloomiest hour. The well-known ability and thorough honesty of the leaders were acknowledged by all, even by those who most widely differed from them, whether Old Irelanders or Orangemen; while the openness of their statement of principles, and their eloquent and powerful advocacy of Irish rights, enlisted the attention and excited the sympathies of the thinking classes of all denominations and political opinions. A Council was created to administer the affairs of the new party, and sub-committees appointed on Finance, Famine, Public Instruction, Trade, Parliamentary Matters, Elections, etc.; upon which prominent places were held by such men as O'Brien, Duffy, Dillon, Bryan, Martin, Mitchel, McGee, McCarthy, Richard O'Gorman, Sr., Richard O'Gorman, Jr., Pigott, Barry, Lawlor, Crean, Reilly, McManus, Doheny, Dr. Cane, Lane, Comyn, Houghton, etc., with appropriate secretaries. The permanent meeting-rooms of the Council were at No. 9, D'Olier St., Dublin, and the Music Hall, one of the most spacious buildings in the city, was usually selected for the semi-monthly public meetings. No sooner had the proceedings of the meeting in the Rotundo been made public, than a large number of persons, including men of all ranks in life, signified their desire to become members of the Confederation; and subscriptions poured in from all quarters, though no pecuniary qualification was fixed for membership.

The first attempt of the young organization was bold, and, though not as successful as was hoped, had yet a wonderful moral effect on the nation. Early in February a vacancy occurred in the representation of Galway by the resignation of Valentine Blake, and two candidates appeared to claim the suffrages of the "City of the Tribes." One was James Henry Monaghan, lately so infamous in Ireland for his brutality and partisanship as one of her Majesty's judges, who was supported by his own party, the Whigs, and by the Tories: the other being an independent Repealer,

Anthony O'Flaherty. The council of the Confederation immediately issued a stirring address to the Repealers of Galway, in which they said:—

"We do not presume to suggest a candidate for your suffrages—you will choose for yourselves. One thing only we ask of you—to vote for no Whig, for no Tory, for none but a pledged and determined Repealer. This, Repealers of Galway, all Irishmen are entitled to demand at your hands—that you send no nominee of an English government to inform his employers that his constituency, for their part, have repented the pledge of '45, have revoked the vows of '45, and are content to accept some paltry, foreign patronage, instead of the blessings, the pride, and the security of an Irish Legislature.

"You will forgive us if we seem for an instance to doubt the fate of your election. But there is a painful and shameful rumor abroad: that an official of the English government dares to hope for the votes of Galway Repealers; an officer of that government which has starved the poor and impoverished the rich—that government which declares that it will resist to the death the attainment of the national independence which we have all sworn to win. Think, Repealers of Galway, of your countrymen most foully murdered by the blasting Union.

"Let Galway be saved for Ireland; and rely on the zealous assistance of this Confederation in securing the eturn of any true Repealer."

Mr. O'Flaherty was not a member of the Confederation; but notwithstanding that he still adhered to the old Association, being a man of patriotic views and opposed to place-hunting, the Council resolved to follow up their proclamation by sending a deputation to Galway to arouse the people into action. The effect of this step was thus described in the Limerick and Clare *Examiner*:

"The Repeal party put forth its strength in a marked and decisive manner. For the past week meetings were held each night in the committee rooms and the theatre, at which the most soul-stirring addresses were delivered by the members of the deputation of the Irish Confederation, whose sincere and untiring exertions on this trying occasion cannot be too highly appreciated. Messrs. O'Gorman, Michael J. Barry, T. F. Meagher and J. B. Dillon, are the men to whom in a great measure may be attributed the enthusiastic ardor which pervades all ranks of the Galwegians at present. Our reporters, on their arrival, found the court-house crowded to suffocation. In one of the galleries, Mr. O'Flaherty and his friends mustered in great numbers, resting their hopes of success, not on the tinsel of office or assurances of those comfortable births, which seem to captivate not a few of the opposite party; but in the glorious, the noble, and the chivalrous principle of national redemption, the principle of Ireland's right to native legislation.

On the other side were arrayed Mr. Monaghan and the apostate Repealers, many of whom, though members of the Association, openly sided with the government candidate. The body of the court was crammed by the visitors, the tried, the unshrinking, frieze-coated Repealers: the cheering was so loud and continuous, that the sheriff was unable for a considerable time to procure a hearing for the candidates. Much confusion was created by a drunken banditti of forty or fifty degraded mercenaries from Claddagh, who were content to barter their freedom for some petty consideration. With this exception, the great body of the people were on the side of nationality."

The election, however, was gained by the Whig candidate through the aid of John O'Connell's Repealers, by a majority of *four*, but the people of the west recognized the treachery of the followers of that person; and to this day they have ample cause to rue the choice which their chief city made in that eventful struggle. "You saw the men who voted for the Repeal candidate," said Meagher in one of his thrilling harangues during the election: "did they register their votes under the sabres of the hussars? No; they voted for their country, and were, therefore, under no obligations to the liveried champions of the English flag. They went up to the hustings like honest citizens, and were protected, not by the musket of the soldier, but by the arm of the God of Hosts. Their souls were as untrammelled as their limbs, and recording their votes, they were distinguished for the manliness which men who love freedom can alone exhibit. They voted like men who knew well that the scheme of the Whigs is to soothe this country into degradation, and they looked like men who scorned to be soothed for that purpose—scorned the vile scheme that would prostrate this country by patronage—scorned the vile scheme that would perpetuate the Union by making it prolific in small boons."

The Confederation continued daily to receive new accessions, some from the ranks of the landholders, but the majority belonged to a class of men who, amid all the horrors of the plague and famine, still had faith in Ireland's future, who read books and newspapers and formed their own political opinions. These were the tradesmen of the towns and the tenant farmers of the rural districts—the bone and sinew, the hope and trust of the land. In promoting this good work, in spreading broadcast the sterling views of the Confederates, and in meeting and refuting the arguments of their enemies, the *Nation* was preëminent and untiring. Still, though its own course was becoming more and more popular, as that of Conciliation Hall was becoming weak and distasteful, it did not relinquish the attempt to fuse all nationalists in one common array against the common oppressor. In April, 1857, an article appeared in its columns, which excited general attention and carried conviction to the minds of many doubtful or wavering Repealers. A few short extracts will be sufficient to show the gravity of the Irish question at this time, and the willingness of the organ of the Confederacy to yield everything possible for the sake of Union.

"There is one resource adequate to our emergency—we believe there is only one : a convocation of our best and wisest Irishmen, to determine how the nation may be saved. Not a new Rotundo meeting to be adulated at home and spat upon abroad, but an assembly that shall be spat upon nowhere; being fit to act as well as to speak. An assembly full of a deep and grave sense of our terrible condition; and which, representing all the interests of the country, the aristocracy, the gentry, the clergy, the professional and mercantile classes, the tenant farmers and the artisans, shall feel itself competent to speak with plenipotentiary authority for this Irish nation."

. . . .

"A national Assembly, then, is our only resource. The ways and means of action which we have suggested may be impolitic or ineffective. Wiser and better plans may exist, of which we know nothing. We stand upon no details. We insist upon no more than the moral necessity of taking counsel together, and doing whatever may seem best to the assembled wisdom of the country. But to act has become essential to our national life, now—now—now—now—or never. If the country do not feel this instinctively and without bidding, as men in a sinking ship fly to the boats, nothing is before us but hopeless ruin."

. . . .

"Mr. John O'Connell asks for a reunion of the Repeal party. Surely, surely, if it be upon some basis of action, some centre like this, round which hope and purpose may rally. And the Conservative press, the *Warder* and the *Packet*, which have preached nationality; and the *Mail* and the *Dublin University*, which have threatened it,—now, if they meant honestly, their time for action is come. The landlords, it is affirmed, are ready for such a movement as we have indicated, if the press in which they trust would counsel it. If they are indeed ready, all the interests in the state may still be saved, and our nation win the holiest and most peaceful triumph in history. If not—if they still falter, still scheme, and still look to their own selfish interests alone, they are doomed of God; and their class—the very men now dallying with our fate—will be trampled under the feet of the English Minister or of the Irish Parliament."

Meanwhile the Council of the Irish Confederation were diligently at work, perfecting its organization, extending its ramifications throughout the country by means of Repeal reading-rooms or clubs, and furnishing, through its committees, much valuable information on the progress of the Famine, the Land Tenure, Manufactures and Industry, Parliamentary Proceedings, Emigration, and other topics of general interest. They also held public meetings semi-monthly in Dublin, at which large numbers of the citizens and gentlemen from the provinces, in sympathy with the movement, were wont to attend. At first the speakers at those meetings were assailed by the mob which had attempted to intimidate the *Remonstrants;* but it was invariably repulsed by the Confederates, till by degrees public opinion became so strongly in favor of freedom of speech, that the champions of moral force were compelled to desist. One of the most important of those meetings was held in April, and was remarkable, not only for the number and enthusiasm of attendants, but for a speech of Charles Gavan Duffy, the first of any importance ever delivered by him in public.

Duffy was, and is, a remarkable man, and in his own sphere one of the ablest that this or any other century has produced in Ireland. In early life he went from his northern home to Dublin, a stranger with but a few shillings in his pocket, with nothing to recommend him but a plain, solid, primary education, sound common-sense and an unconquerable will. For several years he labored in a subordinate capacity on one of the metropolitan newspapers, working hard at his desk for a trifling pittance, and devoting his spare hours, usually spent by young men of his age in pleasure, to study and self-improvement. He subsequently engaged himself as editor of the Belfast *Vindicator*, which became under his management one of the best and most spiritedly conducted papers in Ireland. In 1842, when in his twenty-sixth year, he became editor-in-chief, and, with Davis and Dillon, joint-proprietor of the *Nation*, relations which he continued to hold to that remarkable journal till its suppression by the government in the summer of 1848. As an editor, it is no exaggeration to say that we have had no writer of the English language, in his time, who could be counted his superior, and even very few his equals. Strong, robust, didactic English flowed fluently from his pen, not as a bubbling stream dancing and sparkling, only to be enjoyed momentarily and forgotten; nor as a half-turbid rhetorical torrent, that brings neither persuasion nor conviction; but like a rapid, broad, and limpid river which holds its course, irresistibly bearing along on its ample bosom many an argosy freighted with deep thoughts, clear ideas, and profound reasons. Without for a moment detracting from the merits of his gifted associates, we may be allowed to say that to him, more than to any one man, was due the great success and potency of the *Nation* from the very beginning. His wise counsels governed its course, and his strong, almost abrupt, force and patriotism inspired its editorial columns, and even sometimes lent grace to its lighter literary attractions.

As a judge of human nature in the individual, as a patron of young struggling men, as a political organizer, he was far above most of his cotemporaries; in the latter quality, particularly, he was so preëminently an adept, that his advice and views were highly prized, and freely acknowledged by O'Connell in his best days, and were of incalculable benefit to the new Confederation from its very inception. Like most men who think deeply and are accustomed to shape the course of others from their closets, Duffy had never paid much attention to oratory, and it was only as a matter of duty that he could ever be induced to address an audience. On the occasion, however, of the April meeting, a very important resolution was to be offered, requesting " O'Brien and the other Irish members of all parties henceforth to withdraw altogether from parliament, and to take measures for serving the country at home," and Duffy was requested to propose it. In compliance with this request, he, in the course of a long and impressive speech, said :—

" Is it strange, then, that the Council of the Confederation has come to the resolution of asking you to call upon the Irish members to quit that parliament and take their stand at home, among their own people? We have prayed to the deaf ears of parliament long enough. Wherever succor and redemption are to be had, it is clear enough that they are not to be had there. There is but one place we can find them—there is but one place we have a right to look for them— in ourselves. England at this hour is teeming with wealth and plenty, yet it is not alleged that she possesses any natural advantages that we do not share. She does not starve. Her people do not die in myriads, or fly with averted eyes from her shore. They prosper at home, and glory in the home which shelters and protects them. O friends! has your land no natural rights? Is there some ordinance of God by which we, living in the same latitudes and under the same skies, must see our people die of hunger and nakedness? Oh, infamy! are we to ask this question forever? Let us at least not blaspheme Providence; let us not even blame England: the fault is not England's, but our own. It is the right of this people, and their sacred duty, to protect themselves against all aggressors on the face of the earth, come they east or west, over the broad Atlantic, or across the British Channel. And surely the time has come, while we still suffer under one calamity and await another, to determine the cause of our misery and to take some sure measures for our protection."

Messrs. Mitchel, Doheny, Reilly, McGee, O'Gorman, Jr., Coyne, and Rev. C. P. Meehan, also, spoke at this great meeting. The latter, the pastor of S.S. Michael and John's, Dublin, as distinguished for his erudition as for his charity and zealous devotion to the poor, said in the course of his remarks:— "Look abroad!—wherever there was not provincialism there were manufactures. Need he point to France, Belgium, or glorious America? Let them turn their eyes then to home—let them go to the liberties and into the lanes and alleys of the city of

Dublin, and here he would take leave to state, from his own personal knowledge, that no person was thoroughly acquainted with the misery and fetid disease of these localities, with the exception of the medical attendants, the clergymen, and, in thousands of instances, the Sisters of Charity. This misery, this total absence of manufactures —this total inertness in the mechanics—their pining, haggard aspect—the distress of their families—all these things could be traced as the result of the absence of domestic legislation." The report alluded to was presented by McGee, and was a very exhaustive relation of the state of Irish manufactures and trade. He closed his speech by the following practical advice:—

"Let us alter our condition at home. Let us see what relics of our old prosperity are left us—let us vow to each other to reward the industry of our people—in trade, in mechanics, or in letters. Free Trade and the Famine—two events which have occurred since 1840-- will give this important movement motives and means which the old movement could not have had. If we are determined to stay at home, let it be to help each other, not to destroy. If we will not abandon Ireland, in God's name let us drive famine and bigotry and disunion out. Let us labor to create prosperity, not from the mean motive of hatred to England, but for the better one of justice to our children and our race. Let us cultivate the good-will of other states—let us deserve other men's respect—let us win the approval of our own consciences; but, above all and before all, let us try to deserve the blessings of that God who placed us here, with feelings, appetites, hopes, and fears, and who never intended that his Irish children should live under the ban, and die of the natural wants He gave them."

CHAPTER XI.

An American-Irish Banquet—Richard O'Gorman, Jr.—A truce again proposed—O'Brien in the Confederation—A disgraceful scene in Conciliation Hall—Rev. Mr. McHugh—Death of O'Connell—Its effects on the people—Fate of Conciliation Hall—The *Nation* on the future—Election in Cork a Confederate victory.

SUCH were the sentiments and aims of the Confederates; and it is no wonder that, sound and national as they were, they were found gradually permeating all classes of the people. The members of the Council on their part neglected no proper occasion to reiterate and develop them in all possible forms. An opportunity of this sort was presented on the 4th of May, '47, when a banquet was given in Dublin in honor of Captain Clark and the crew of the American ship *Victor*, which had come freighted with a portion of the generous offerings of the citizens of the United States to the Irish people. A large company sat down, and some good speeches were delivered on the occasion—O'Gorman, Jr.'s, and Meagher's being among the number. The former, in responding to the toast, "Peace and Prosperity to our Native Land," said:—

"We have had public meetings and public speeches enough. The voice of our sorrow has crossed the Atlantic. We have threatened, we have promised—and I confess I feel almost ashamed in speaking before that gentleman—I feel myself ashamed of my position as an Irishman—I feel that I belong to a race the most abject, the most degraded, the most servile of any that has ever blotted the face of the earth. We are in the habit, in this land, of praising one another, of saying that the Irish people are the finest, the bravest, the boldest in the world. We are no such thing. I will tell you what we are. We have borne more suffering, we have tamely borne more degradation, we have broken more vows, than any other nation I ever read of. And now, gentlemen, when you drink with enthusiasm the toast of 'Prosperity to Ireland,' let me tell you this, that in my heart and soul I believe that the cause of the absence of that prosperity is not so much the misgovernment of any other country, as a want of self-reliance and honest exertion among yourselves. If you are fit to be free, if you are honest men, when you hear the toast, 'Prosperity to Ireland,' remember that that prosperity depends upon yourselves—remember it is yours to seek it—it is yours to win it. And if you want to know how it is to be won, ask Captain Clark of America. If you want to know how Irish prosperity is to be obtained, read the history of American Independence."

These utterances, these homely, but unpalatable truths, were quite in keeping with the younger O'Gorman's character. At that time he was in the full flush of his early manhood, thoroughly educated, full of manliness and devotion to the cause of Ireland; his proud spirit could not brook the degradation and uncomplaining squalor which every day he beheld in the streets of his native city. He was then speaking under the very roof that had two short years before reverberated to the cheers of thousands who had signed the Rotundo pledge, and within gunshot of Conciliation Hall in which it had been so shamefully violated. O'Gorman was as eloquent as he was fearless, and his fine presence and melodious accents added a charm to everything he said. But he was not content to please; he preferred to speak plain truths. On the 16th of the previous March, at a meeting of the citizens of Dublin presided over by the Lord Mayor, in moving the following resolution, he bluntly remarked, in reply to a previous speaker: "Mr. Fitzgibbon has suggested that the measures of government may have been adopted under an infatuation. I believe there is no infatuation. I hold a very different opinion on the subject. I think the British government are doing what they intend to do." He then, to the astonishment of many, moved:—

"That for purposes of temporary relief, as well as permanent improvement, the one great want and demand of Ireland is, that Foreign Legislators and Foreign Ministers shall no longer interfere in the management of her affairs."

It was passed. O'Gorman had long been a prominent member of the Repeal Committee, but from the secession he shared the fortunes of his friends, and became one of the most trusted, popular, and useful members of the Confederation.

In the early part of May, another effort was made to bring about a reconciliation between the dissevered members of the Repealers. The Rev. Mr. McHugh sent a letter to O'Gorman, which was laid before the Council, accompanied by a copy of a resolution of the Committee of the Repeal Association, authorizing him to request a conference between the leading members of the Confederation and of the Association, to adjust the differences between Repealers. O'Brien, Duffy, Mitchel, Dillon, McGee, O'Gorman, Jr., Doheny, and Meagher were, in compliance with this request, appointed, with definite instructions. Both delegations having met on the 4th of May, it was proposed by those acting on the part of the Confederation that the two Repeal organizations should be dissolved and an entirely new one formed, as the first step to a hearty and efficient reunion. This was objected to on the part of the Association, and in consequence the negotiation failed. At the public meeting of the Irish Confederation which followed this abortive attempt, O'Brien, chairman of the delegation, in explaining the propositions laid before the conference, said :—

"With regard to the policy of the new Association, I candidly tell you that we thought there was no hope for Repeal if this country were to become a nation of place-hunters. I do not believe that any nation ever won its liberties, or ever will win its liberties, by place-hunting. We, the Repeal party, consider ourselves in a position of antagonism to all parties, particularly English parties opposed to Repeal; and I should like to know what a chance there would be of winning any contest in which the combatants were to begin by asking favors from those on the other side? We are told forsooth,—and this is the pretext—that if the places be obtained by Repealers, the hands of Repealers will be strengthened, and they can wield the power which they so acquire against their benefactors. Gentlemen, I will not ask an assembly of Irishmen what they think of the chivalry, the generosity, and the magnanimity of that sentiment. But we have the advantage of having this question tested by experience; and I should like to know the individual who, after having received a place from the government, has afterwards continued an ardent, zealous Repealer? I should like to know whether, since this doctrine has been preached, Repealers can think they occupy the position in the eyes of mankind that they did before?"

As an instance of how widely John O'Connell differed from the Confederates on this very vital point, we quote from a speech of his delivered in Conciliation Hall, a few weeks previously, on place-hunting, the following paragraph:—

"I have, at the instance of private individuals of high worth and respectability—very many of them clergymen and dignitaries in the Catholic Church—recommended respectable and meritorious persons to the notice of government; as was, in fact, a part of my duty as a member of parliament not in direct opposition on all points to that government."

The full significance of this debasing admission will be better understood, when we recollect that every paid official of the government was not only prohibited from becoming a member of the Repeal party, and from voting at any parliamentary election, but that his simple appearance at a Repeal meeting or banquet was considered sufficient cause for his discharge.

The scene in the Association, which took place at the general meeting following the failure of the negotiations, defies description, and, considering the characters of the parties engaged, was altogether unlooked for. It is thus sketched in the papers of the day: Rev. Mr. McHugh, having endorsed the opinion of the necessity of dissolving the Association, proceeded to advocate the formation of a new one, in imitation of O'Connell's tactics during the Emancipation agitation. Amid much unseemly interruption John O'Connell at length stepped forward :—

Mr. John O'Connell—"No, no, pardon me. Allow me to set the reverend gentleman right. If the bishops of Ireland—if the clergy of Ireland—if the people of Ireland and Daniel O'Connell consent to it (great cheering)——"

Rev. Mr. McHugh—"I object to that, sir; I object to the introduction of——"

A voice—"Three cheers for O'Connell." (Great cheering.)

Rev. Mr. McHugh—"I must object totally and strongly to the dragging of the names of the venerated prelacy and clergy of Ireland into this association. I am not much wrong in saying that no man has a right to drag the names of that venerated body into our discussions, as Mr. John O'Connell has done. (Approbation.) I request, sir, that you will be more abstemious in future in acting as you have done on this occasion, by using the names of the Catholic hierarchy and clergy without their permission. I have good reason for stating publicly that there is great dissatisfaction abroad with regard to that point. There is too much liberty taken in dragging the names of our clergy into every political movement. (No, no.) How can you expect Protestant gentlemen of high character, of strong Protestant feeling, who, at the same time, are deeply imbued with the principles of nationality, to work with you if the practice of dragging religious subjects into your debates is not discontinued? (A voice—You are right.) The Repealers were divided amongst themselves. There were New Irelanders and Old Irelanders. They were both talking about Repeal, yet both impotent—not advancing one step. The English Ministry did but laugh at them. There was nothing now but Old and Young Ireland abusing this or that man. They talked of dissolving. Why, they were defunct already. (Loud cries of No, no.) To say 'no' costs nothing, but he said yes. (Cheers.) Many respectable gentlemen had been amongst them. He did not see them there. Where were they? They were not connected with them—and without them they could do nothing. It was stated at the conference that, if there were a reconciliation, it would only be conditional until Mr. O'Connell returned. (No, no, from Mr. J. O'Connell and other members.) He said yes, and the statement was made in the presence of the sixteen gentlemen: then, if reconciliation were to be only conditional, what was the use of bringing Mr. O'Brien and the other respectable gentlemen there?" (Hissing and confusion).

The chairman implored the meeting to hear Mr. McHugh out.

The Rev. Mr. McHugh—"Indeed they won't!".

The Chairman—"I do not think that the rev. gentleman can complain of not being heard, considering the concession that has been made to him."

The Rev. Mr. McHugh proceeded to say that he did not think such a course to patch up a union, until they had the pleasure of seeing Mr. O'Connell amongst them, was candid. He did not expect it. He would submit that the conference had not been carried out in a fair spirit. Mr. O'Brien had proposed that the accounts should be published. He agreed with him. What had become of all their money? (Cheers and hisses.) He questioned no man's honesty, they were all honorable men; but every public body should account to the public for the public money. (Cheers.) The rev. gentleman, in conclusion, called upon Mr. J. O'Connell not to keep splitting hairs with the Young Ireland party, but to reorganize the Association, which, at the eleventh hour, might still stay the torrent of bad legislation.

While this unseemly exhibition of narrow-minded prejudice was being enacted, and while the name of the great Liberator was being made the watchword of faction and bigotry by his unworthy son, the soul of that illustrious man was struggling to free itself from its earthly tenement, and soar to the judgment-seat where all the deeds of this life are sure to meet at last their just reward; and where alone the motives and springs of human action are truly known.

Overpowered by the terrible calamities, to which the people for whom he had so long labored were exposed; disheartened by the factious and selfish conduct of those even of his own blood, and disgusted with the treachery and bad faith of the Whigs; worn down by years and enfeebled by sickness, he left Parliament early in the session, and by the advice of his physicians retired to Hastings. Not feeling much benefited by the change of air, he was recommended to try the south of Europe; and on the 21st of April, accompanied by Rev. Dr. Miley, his chaplain, he set out for Rome, *via* Paris. In the latter city he was attended by the most eminent medical men, who united in pronouncing his malady, though dangerous, not necessarily fatal. In the French capital, also, he received the marked attention of such distinguished men as the Archbishop, Montalembert, de Laroche Jaquelin, and others. The members of the Electoral Committee for the defence of religious liberty, consisting of some of the most eminent men of the day, likewise showed him all the respect and sympathy possible under the painful circumstances. On the 29th, he resumed his route to Rome by the way of

Orleans, Lyons, and Marseilles, his youngest son and two French doctors having been added to his escort. Everywhere on his journey he received the greatest marks of respect, and enthusiastic multitudes accompanied his steps throughout. From Civita Vecchia he endeavored to push on to the Eternal City, as fast as his sinking health would permit, but was obliged to halt at Genoa, where on the 15th of May, 1847, he breathed his last.

It would be difficult adequately to describe the profound sensation of sorrow which the news of O'Connell's death produced among all classes in Ireland. Those who had neither liked him politically, nor followed him in his days of triumph, vied with the sincere Repealers yet left in the Association, and with the Confederates, always the warm admirers of his genius and patriotism, in tokens of genuine grief for the great loss which Ireland, Europe, nay Christendom itself, had sustained in the demise of one of the most gigantic intellects that ever planned, wrought, and struggled for the civil and religious rights of mankind. Whatever faults he might have had, were ignored; whatever unkind word or arbitrary sentence he might have let fall in unguarded moments, was forgotten. Faction itself, the bitter, fell spirit of disunion and jealousy, was for a time hushed—no, not completely hushed, for the miserable few who then guided the councils of the once great Association he had founded, and the scarcely less contemptible crew that believed in them, raised the cry that it was the conduct of the "Young Irelanders" which had hastened his death; when it was as well known to them, as it is now to the whole world, that the seeds of the disease of which he eventually died, were planted long anterior to the difference which sprung up in 1846, and in all probability may be traced back to his imprisonment two years previously. To such an extent, and to give additional credence to the foul calumny, was this petty spite carried, that, when the members of the Confederate Council signified their intention of accompanying the body to its last resting-place in Glasnevin, permission was refused by John O'Connell on behalf of himself and the other members of the family.

With the death of the great chieftain, the Repeal Association, which had for some months been living solely on the charm of his name, became a helpless, inane institution—a training school for office-seekers and amateur traitors, and finally lapsed into oblivion. Tom Steele, one of the few honest, if not the wisest of its members, first left; then came a scramble for obscure government appointments at home and abroad, and a few years afterwards the arch dissembler and prime disturber, John O'Connell, passed away almost unnoticed, with a pair of eleemosynary epaulets and with the rank of captain in the British—militia.

The conduct of the Irish Confederates under these trying circumstances was singularly delicate and dignified. Their sorrow was deep and true, and they expressed it as men should do, not by idle repinings and vain lamentations, but by resolving anew to carry out the plans their great exemplar had laid down, and for the fulfilment of which he had toiled so energetically till the whisperings of false friends and the lures of the Whigs had induced him partially to abandon them. At their meetings his name was always mentioned with profound respect, and his memory was embalmed in prose and verse. They in truth revered his great virtues, admired his comprehensive mind, and loved the hand that had dealt such heavy blows against England, albeit it had been raised sometimes against themselves. Said the *Nation*, when the news of O'Connell's demise reached Ireland:

That that Future includes liberty for Ireland, is beyond question. But how it will be worked out, by what agencies and in what time, depends on many conditions. If we make the tomb of the lost Liberator an altar on which to lay down our personal wrongs and party differences, the work he projected may soon be accomplished. If the country remain broken and irritated, a prey to petty factions, a stage for rival ambitions, the way may be long, obscure, and bloody. He in his vigorous youth might, single-handed, have reduced such a chaos to order; and so, happily, may men of less power, with less labor, if they work with one heart.

There is no hope of another O'Connell; but let us remember that all modern revolutions have been effected by coöperation, and do the thing we are competent to do. If he had a successor adequate to succeed him, he would be no servile copy. O'Connell did not resemble O'Neil, Swift, or Grattan. The strength of each was that he brought to his task capacities and sympathies suited to his own time. And so a new O'Connell would need and would possess new powers and resources in harmony with the means and wants of the country. Perhaps, in the honest coöperation of many minds, the nearest possible approximation to this ideal may be found. May Heaven send it in some shape, that our path to liberty may not lie through revolution and anarchy."

It was in this spirit of conciliation and good feeling that the Confederates took part in the Cork election of July to fill the place of the late member, the lost Liberator. The contest was carried on by an Englishman named Leander, in the Tory and Whig interest, and Dr. Maurice Power, a member of the Repeal Association, pledged, however, against place-hunting and the wiles of Whiggery, strongly fortified in that faith by a series of resolutions passed by his fellow-citizens. To assist Dr. Power, and as a representative of the Confederation, O'Brien made his appearance at the hustings amid the wildest applause. At the request of the people he addressed the vast audience in a speech of some hours, advocating and explaining in their order the principles which should govern true nationalists. The election which lasted several days ended in the triumphant return of the Repeal candidate. Said the Cork *Examiner*, in announcing the result :—

"We cannot, before we conclude, avoid giving utterance to the gratification we felt at the unanimity and union of Old and Young Irelanders on this occasion. It was more than many an anxious friend to nationality dared to anticipate, and as much as the most ardent lover of his country could desire. It establishes, notwithstanding the personal dispute in Dublin, this most heart-cheering and important fact, that past estrangement does not mar concord at a crisis, and that, however Repealers may differ on matters of secondary moment, all agree on the great principle."

With this additional moral victory on their banner, the Confederates prepared to take an active part in the approaching general elections; and while avoiding dictation or putting forward their own candidates, they resolutely set their face against all *pseudo* Repealers who would not pledge themselves against seeking the patronage of either English party.

CHAPTER XII.

The General Elections of 1847.—J. O'Connell withdraws from Dublin—O'Brien reëlected for Limerick—Meagher in Waterford—The Repeal members—Grattan on the Famine—The Irish Council—The Confederate Clubs—Division in the Confederation—John Mitchel—Meeting in Dublin—The French Revolution of 1848.—Its effect on Ireland—Deputation to Paris—Arrests—Transportation of Mitchel—End of the old *Nation*.

PREVIOUS to the general elections which took place late in the summer of 1847, the Council of the Confederation issued an address to the people, asking them to withhold their votes from Whig and Tory alike, and not to support any person who claimed to be a Repealer unless he was willing to pledge himself against place-hunting. They did not put forward their own members as candidates, but expressed their willingness to aid by all their power the election of sincere members of the Association, as they had done at Galway and Cork, on the principle, "that the first qualification for an Irish representative was, that he should be zealously devoted to Irish Independence; and second, that he should be of personal integrity—one who would not accept or solicit office." To carry out these views, they sent to different parts of the country some of their best speakers, such as O'Gorman, Meagher, and Doheny, wherever their presence was most needed.

John O'Connell was the first person to feel the effect of the strict and salutary test of fidelity to Ireland. He had become notorious as a solicitor of offices, and, without word of apology or regret for so doing, had offered himself as a candidate for Dublin. At a meeting of the Council soon after, it was resolved to recommend the Confederates of the capital to vote against him. The newspapers in the interest of the Castle and Conciliation Hall took occasion, upon alluding to this resolution, to assert that many of the Council dissented from it. Whereupon letters appeared from O'Gorman, O'Reilly, McGee, and O'Brien, fully endorsing the cause of the Council: the latter, in particular, was most emphatic. Speaking for the Confederates, he said:—

"We believe that it is utterly impossible for an individual to be at the same time a true Irish patriot, and a time-serving dependant—a fawning sycophant of an English minister. We believe that the character, not only of the Irish members, but also of the whole Irish nation, has been irretrievably degraded in the opinion of mankind by the pliant subserviency exhibited during the present year by many who call themselves Repealers. We believe that the national interests of our country have been sacrificed to the private interests of individuals."

After this the friends of John O'Connell withdrew his name.

O'Brien was solicited by his Limerick constituency to allow his name to be put in nomination. This he refused on the ground that Powell, who was intended to be his colleague, though a Repealer, "had avowed himself to be a place-hunter," and that Mr. Monsell, though otherwise qualified, was not a Repealer at all; adding, however: "If the electors of the county feel disposed to return me, without expecting that I should commit myself to the support of either of the other candidates, I shall continue to serve them as their representative to the best of my ability." The electors accepted his conditions and returned him triumphantly.

Thomas Francis Meagher was requested to stand for his native city; and as the Waterford men could not find a member of the Repeal Association independent enough to forswear place-begging, he reluctantly consented. His opponents were Costelloe, one of the meanest sort of Whig-Repealers, and Henry W. Barron, a gentleman of high standing. The latter was elected; for though Meagher was highly popular with the unfranchised masses, the select minority who were privileged to vote were not yet educated up to the true national standard. The young orator had, however, what he valued more than a seat in the English Commons, a fair and full chance to explain to his fellow-townsmen the objects and aims of the Confederation in his own eloquent and irresistible manner.

The total result of the general elections,

as far as Ireland was concerned, was of little advantage to that unfortunate country; for, though more Repealers were chosen, they were generally of the worst kind, such as J. O'Connell, Reynolds, and Somers, all time-servers and Whigs in slim disguise. The labors of the Confederates were, however, not thrown away; for a few independent nationalists were sent to London to save, if for nothing else, the country from utter disgrace.

In the latter part of September, a body called the Irish Council held its first meeting under the presidency of Lord Cloncurry. The attendance was numerous, and consisted of several members of parliament, noblemen, landlords, professional gentlemen, and farmers. They were of all shades of opinion: Confederates and old Irelanders, Whigs and Tories of the more independent stripe, and individuals of no fixed opinions; their ostensible object being to take into consideration the grievances of Ireland and provide a remedy for them. Several meetings of this body were held during the autumn and winter of 1847-8, but no practical results followed. There was one advantage, however, derived from those miscellaneous gatherings. They were attended by many of the prominent members of the Confederation, who, in the usual course of business, never failed to impress on the minds of their audiences their own spirit of earnest, untiring endeavor to regain the lost independence of the nation. Many converts to their views were made in this way; some of them like Lords Ross and Wallscourt, R. D. Ireland, Ferguson, and others, being men of substance and brains.

The Irish Confederation did not place much confidence either in the Irish Council or the so-called " Repeal delegation" to Parliament. They were fully alive to the fact that, if any good was to be effected, it must be through the people and by the people. Henry Grattan, M. P., the son of the illustrious man of '82, struck the proper key-note when he said at a meeting of the Irish members :—

"If you address the Lord Lieutenant, you address an individual who has no power—if you address Downing street, you address a body that has no heart—but if you address the Irish people, you address men who have both hands and hearts. If some active measures be not taken to rouse the country from the peril in which it is placed, I am determined to write as strong a letter as I can to the people of Ireland; for I will not stand quietly by and see the people dying about me in hundreds—nor will I consent to act the part of a gravedigger, and run the risk of bringing fever into my house, which I was almost brought to last year, for any minister or any queen. It is impossible to go on in this way —I say it as a landed gentleman, and a man of feeling. So dreadful were the narratives of human suffering which were received by the Central Relief Committee in their rooms in College Green, that I have seen Irish gentlemen—some of the first men in the country—turn their faces to the wall in order that others could not see the tears falling from their eyes. Again I repeat, we cannot continue to go on in this way; and, in my opinion, if you wish to influence and arouse the country, you should address the Irish people."

What Mr. Grattan proposed was already being practically carried out by the Council of the Confederation. But they did not limit themselves to empty and meaningless appeals. They knew well that the strength of all political parties lies in thorough organization, and they therefore adopted the system of national clubs, each being in its proper sphere an independent body, but in direct communication with the general Council. Each club was to have its own officers elected by the members, its library, reading-room, and, when possible, its gymnasium; its regular nights of meeting, reports, debates and lectures on political, scientific, and literary subjects; and it was hoped, not without reason, when the cities, towns, villages and hamlets of the four provinces were thus overspread by a network of such societies—all working for the same purpose and obeying a single authority—the time would be near at hand for the whole mass of the people to rise simultaneously and demand justice and the restoration of their pilfered rights. The plan may not have originated with Duffy—for, save in its application to Ireland, it can scarcely be called an original one in any sense—but it is certain that he of all among the Confederates was the most active in advocating its adoption in the Council, and the most energetic in executing it among the people.

Nothing could have better suited his organizing ability, nor could any scheme be devised more aptly calculated to give cohesion and unity to the national movement. In Dublin, where it was first tried, its success was beyond all expectation. Club after club was founded in the city in October, November, and December of 1847, each bearing a distinctive title; such as the "Sarsfield," "Dr. Doyle," "Grattan," "St. Patrick's," "Wolfe Tone," "Curran," and "Emmet," or "Swift" Club; the presidents of which were generally prominent leaders in the Confederation. When the names of Irish patriots were exhausted, others were added, such as the "Medical Students' Club," the "Mercantile Assistants'," &c., &c. On certain nights one or other of these societies held an open meeting in its rooms, when lectures were delivered or debates took place on some public topic of general interest; and by this means were constantly brought together, for the interchange of opinions, men of different walks of life, who, under ordinary circumstances, would never have met or known one another. The moral effect of these local associations was only second to their political utility. They were composed for the most part of young men, whose evenings, particularly in cities and large towns, were too often spent in frivolous or deleterious amusements; but, by gathering them in where good books were plentiful and pleasant companionship always to be found, it not only crystallized their opinions, but removed them from many excesses and temptations.

The example of the metropolis was soon followed by the provincial towns, and everywhere clubs began to spring up, founded on the same plan. Deputations, also, were occasionally sent from the Council to Cork, Belfast, Limerick, Kilkenny, and other centres of population, to awaken the attention of the people to the necessity of exertion, as well as to explain to them the principles upon which the Confederates proposed to work for the general good. Thus, though the people were sorely afflicted by continued famine and increasing pestilence, and depleted by a vast hegira of fugitives across the Atlantic; though the great Association founded by O'Connell had degenerated into worse than imbecility; and the various attempts of well-meaning but impracticable men, such as mainly composed the Irish Council, the Agricultural Society, and the National Council, had come to naught,—the new year opened to the surviving nationalists with something like hopefulness and trust in the future. Twelve months more of uninterrupted organization, it was hoped, and the whole country would be one congeries of clubs, willing and ready at a moment's notice to move at the suggestion of the Confederate Council. The very idea of such a result gave strength to the weak, and confidence to the doubtful and despondent.

The hopes of the nationalists were, however, destined to be nipped in the bud even in their hour of greatest promise, and that, too, by dissension in their own ranks. It began to be generally whispered in the clubs that serious differences of opinion had sprung up in the Confederate Council and among the writers of the *Nation*, on the question of continuing the agitation on the original principles of the Confederation, or of abandoning them in favor of armed resistance to the payment of rents and summary ejectments. Those in favor of the former cause urged that all hope of redress by peaceful means was not exhausted, that the people were neither yet properly organized, nor in a condition to sustain their demands by force, and that any attempt to induce them to do so would be promptly suppressed by the government, and all chance of rescuing the country from her degraded position would be indefinitely postponed. Those who were in favor of a change pleaded the failure of the Irish Council, the passage of the new Coercion bill, which would soon disarm all the people, and the protracted famine; adding that, as the masses would die anyhow, it was better for them to die with arms in their hands than as helpless paupers.

Mitchel, entertaining the latter views, and having severed his connection with the *Nation*, wrote a long explanatory letter to Duffy, dated on the 7th of January, 1848; in which, after clearly stating his reasons for so doing, he thus laid down his own ideas as to the proper course to be pursued by the Confederation:—

"With reference to the future direction which should be given to the energies of the country, and of the Irish Confederation, I desired, in the first place, once for all, to turn men's minds away from the English parliament, and from parliamentary agitation of all kinds. I have made up my mind that, inasmuch as the mass of the people have no franchises, and are not likely to get any; and inasmuch as the constituencies, being very small, very poor, and growing smaller and poorer continually, are so easily gained over by corruption and bribery; and inasmuch as any combination of the 'gentry' with the people is now and henceforth impossible,—that, for all these reasons, any organization for parliamentary or constitutional action would be merely throwing away time and strength, and insuring our own perpetual defeat. Therefore I desired that the *Nation* and the Confederation should rather employ themselves in promulgating sound instruction upon military affairs—upon natural lines of defence which make the island so strong, and the method of making those available—upon the construction and defence of field-works, and especially upon the use of proper arms—not with a view to any immediate insurrection, but in order that the stupid 'legal and constitutional' shouting, voting, and 'agitating,' that have made our country an abomination to the whole earth, should be changed into a deliberate study of the theory and practice of guerilla warfare; and that the true and only method of regenerating Ireland might, in course of time, recommend itself to a nation so long abused and deluded by 'legal' humbug."

Duffy could not consent to the expression of those radical opinions in the *Nation*, holding them to be impracticable and delusive; and hence the retirement of his confrère, and the establishment soon after of a paper called the *United Irishman*. John Mitchel for over two years had been one of the ablest and most original writers of the *Nation*, a good speaker, and had been a prominent member of the old Association and the '82 club. He was one of the founders of the Irish Confederation, and among the most active promoters of its opinions in the Council and elsewhere; and though many of his associates found it difficult to agree with the new policy he had marked out for himself, none doubted the honesty of his convictions or the sincerity of his purpose. He was born in Derry in 1815, and became a practising solicitor in Banbridge before he entered into public life, during which his whole career was marked by strong Presbyterian strictness and rectitude. Had he but lived half a century previous, he would doubtless have been a prominent United Irishman.

The differences of opinion which sprung up in the *Nation* office soon found their way into the Council, and gave rise to long and animated debates. The great majority of the members, however—notably, Duffy, O'Brien, and McGee—were opposed to the abandonment of the existing agitation. On the plea that the Council no longer represented the opinions of the Confederates at large on this question, an appeal to the members generally was demanded and granted. A public debate therefore took place in the Rotundo on the evenings of the 2d, 3d, and 4th of February, in which nearly every prominent Confederate in the city, and many from the provinces, took part. The question was on the following resolutions introduced by O'Brien:—

"Resolved:—That inasmuch as letters published by two members of this Council have brought into question the principles of the Irish Confederation, and have given rise to an imputation that we are desirous to produce a general disorganization of society in this country, and to overthrow social order, we deem it right to place before the public the following fundamental rule, as that which constitutes the basis of action proposed to our fellow-countrymen by the Irish Confederation:

"Rule.

"I. That a society be now formed under the title of 'The Irish Confederation,' for the purpose of protecting our national interests, and obtaining the legislative independence of Ireland, by the force of opinion, by the combination of all classes of Irishmen, and the exercise of all the political, social, and moral influences within our reach.

"II. That under present circumstances the only hope of the liberation of this country lies in a movement in which all classes and creeds of Irishmen shall be fairly represented, and by which the interests of none shall be endangered.

"III. That inasmuch as English legislation threatens

all Irishmen with a common ruin, we entertain a confident hope their common necessities will speedily unite Irishmen in an effort to get rid of it.

"IV. That we earnestly deprecate the expression of any sentiments in the Confederation, calculated to repel or alarm any section of our fellow-countrymen.

"V. That we disclaim, as we have disclaimed, any intention of involving our country in civil war, or of invading the just rights of any portion of its people.

"VI. That the Confederation has not recommended, nor does it recommend, resistance to the payment of rates and rents, but, on the contrary, unequivocally condemns such recommendations.

"VII. That, in protesting against the disarmament of the Irish people, under the Coercion Bill lately enacted, and in maintaining that the right to bear arms, and to use them for legitimate purposes, is one of the primary attributes of liberty, we have had no intention or desire to encourage any portion of the population of this country in the perpetration of crimes, such as those which have recently brought disgrace upon the Irish people; and which have tended, in no trifling degree, to retard the success of our efforts in the cause of national freedom.

"VIII. That to hold out to the Irish people the hope that, in this present broken and divided condition, they can liberate their country by an appeal to arms, and consequently to divert them from constitutional action, would be, in our opinion, a fatal misdirection of the public mind.

"IX. That this Confederation was established to

obtain an Irish parliament, by the combination of classes, and by the force of opinion, exercised in constitutional operations; and that no means of a contrary character can be recommended or promoted through its organization, while its present fundamental rules remain unaltered.

"X. That while we deem it right thus emphatically to disavow the principles propounded in the publications referred to in the resolutions, we at the same time equally distinctly repudiate all right to control the *private opinions* of any member of our body, provided they do not affect the legal or moral responsibility of the Irish Confederation."

This resolution was supported by the mover, by Duffy, Meagher, Dillon, McGee, O'Gorman, Doheny, and a number of leading Confederates; while the amendment, which read as follows, was sustained by Mitchel, Reilly, Martin, and a few others of lesser note :—

Amendment: "That this Confederation does not feel called upon to promote either a condemnation or approval of any doctrines promulgated by any of its members, in letters, speeches, or otherwise; because the seventh fundamental rule of the Confederation expressly provides: 'That inasmuch as the essential bond of union amongst us is the assertion of Ireland's right to an independent legislature, no member of the Irish

Confederation shall be bound to the adoption of any principle involved in any resolution, or promulgated by any speaker in the society, or any journal advocating its policy, to which he has not given his special consent, save only the foregoing fundamental principles of the society.'"

The entire proceedings were conducted with decided ability and becoming gravity, the greatest order and decorum prevailing throughout; and at its termination, upon a vote being taken, it was found that the large majority of the Confederates present sustained the resolution and, of course, rejected the amendment. Thenceforth Mitchel and Reilly ceased all active participation in the Council, but continued to advocate their peculiar views in the columns of the *United Irishman*; Duffy and McGee, with the entire staff of the *Nation*, except one or two, continuing the work of quiet and steady organization of the people in their journal. In the metropolitan clubs, the differences between the leaders had naturally found an echo; but, so far from disturbing their good feeling and harmony, they were impelled to greater exertions, and the number of new clubs that were springing up in the provinces became greater than at any other period. Though personally liked, the course of Mitchel and his friends had little perceptible effect on the aims of the body of the Confederates, the large circulation of the *United Irishman* notwithstanding. It was only later, when the news of the French Revolution of February arrived, that the young men of the country, excited, misled, and misdirected, began to talk of arming and fighting, of rifles and barricades. The commotion excited over all Europe by that event quickly reached Ireland; and thousands, who neither knew how to load, much less to fire, a musket, spoke of nothing but warfare and revolution. They forgot that Dublin was not Paris, that a three days' insurrection there, inaugurated by myriads of armed men, was simply to overthrow a dynasty, not to war against a hostile nation, more populous and infinitely more wealthy than themselves, with fleets, armies, an inexhaustible treasury, and the armed possession of every available portion of their soil. However, the madness of the hour prevailed, and even infected many of the less far-seeing of the members of the Council. From this moment the clubs were fatally doomed. They had been devised to embrace all the people in a political and literary union, and, should future circumstances require, for ulterior objects. They were now turned into mere shows, in which full-grown men babbled, like boys, of shaking the "foundations of the British empire," and boys discoursed learnedly on the "queen of weapons, the pike," and the most improved methods of "appealing to the god of the barricades." It is sorrowful to look back and contemplate how many, otherwise intelligent, sincere, and brave, men allowed themselves to be led astray by the *ignis fatuus* of forcible resistance, at a time when their country, famine-stricken and desolated, was never more powerless, or ignorant of the art of war, and their enemy never so strong by foreign alliances and domestic prosperity.

The *Nation*, true to its instinctive prudence and wisdom, endeavored to repress, as much as possible, this ebullition of empty declamation, but with only partial success. Men of mature thought, who knew so well that the Confederation, though it had won over many individuals to their side, had not yet succeeded in gaining the confidence of the clergy or of the mass of the Repealers, strove with all their might to moderate the ardor of their less experienced associates, but with little practical effect. They were even in some instances carried away in the torrent of excitement.

New fuel was added to the flame by the action of the Confederation on the 15th of March, when an address of congratulation to the French people was adopted. A Committee of three, O'Brien, Meagher, and Hollywood, was sent to Paris to present it to Lamartine; and returned after fulfilling its mission, with fair words and a tricolor flag. O'Brien, on his return, stopped a while in London, and appeared in the House of Commons for the last time. In attempting to address the members, he was assailed with hisses, catcalls, and other unseemly demonstrations of hostility, all of which, however, he bore with unshaken coolness and treated with contempt. The evil fruits of the change of policy on the part of the majority of the Council were soon developed. In March, O'Brien, Meagher, and Mitchel were arrested, and held to bail in Dublin for sedition; and about the same time McGee and Hollywood were taken up in Wicklow on the same charge. The two latter were discharged on the preliminary examination; in the case of O'Brien and Meagher the juries disagreed, but Mitchel, having had a second indictment framed against him under the charge of treason-felony, was tried on the latter, found guilty, and, on the 27th of May, was sentenced to fourteen years' penal servitude.

It was Mitchel's object, it has been alleged, by his bold, able, and very stirring articles in the *United Irishman*, to rouse the country to arms, to raise a direct issue with the Castle authorities, and, by throwing himself into the breach, to bring at once the people and their oppressors face to face in armed array.

If such were his aims, he had sadly mistaken the strength and temper of the people. Dublin at the time was filled with troops; and the Confederates, if they had ever been willing to attempt an insurrection, would have been slaughtered without even the poor satisfaction of being able to make a decent fight. The most noisy, and, of course, the least practical, spoke of the advisability of such a measure, but, as the time for action approached, their numbers dwindled away into a knot of four or five. The Council after this was reduced to twenty-one members, as, being more wieldy and thus rendered more select, it was thought it would exhibit greater sagacity. But the time foreseen by the supporters of O'Brien's resolution and rule in the preceding February had arrived, and the "law" was about to crush the Confederation.

John Martin, who had established the *Felon* as a successor to the *United Irishman*, was arrested on the 8th of July, and on the 19th of August was sentenced to transportation for ten years. Kevin Izod O'Dougherty, and R. D. Williams of the *Tribune*, were also put in prison at the same time; and the former, after three trials being convicted, was, on the 30th of October, also sentenced to a like term of years. Williams was acquitted on a legal technicality. Duffy, the head and front of the Confederacy, was on the same 8th of July lodged in Newgate, but, though three times tried, the government failed to convict him, owing to the refusal of each jury to agree. While in jail and before his trial, the *Nation* was summarily seized by the police, and the property of both publishing and printing office destroyed. Thus ended the first chapter in the history of that remarkable journal, whose last editors, at the moment of its extinction, were two ladies,—Mrs. Dr. Callan (Thornton McMahon), and Miss Elgee, now Lady Wilde, so well known by her *nom de plume* of "Speranza;" and the writer.

Some short time previous to the happening of these events, an attempt was again made to unite all the Repealers in one harmonious whole and upon a common basis, but the project again failed lamentably; and all hope for Ireland, for one generation at least, vanished. As a last resort, and to meet the demands of their Repeal opponents, the Irish Confederation had resolved to abandon its distinctive organization, and help to form a new one on a basis which, it was hoped, would meet the wishes of all sincere nationalists; but the hope was vain. The variance of opinion was so great that no permanent union could be established. The Confederate Council having ceased to exist, the clubs of Dublin and the neighborhood elected a Directory, consisting of Dillon, O'Gorman, McGee, Meagher, and Reilly; but, owing to the general confusion prevailing in the City and the suspension of the *Habeas Corpus*, they had only one meeting, at which it was informally agreed that, while McGee would first proceed to Scotland and then to the North of Ireland, the others should go to the South to join O'Brien and Doheny, the latter of whom, it was reported, had a large number of men already in arms in his native county.

CHAPTER XIII.

Attempts at insurrection in the South—The affairs at Ballingarry—Escape of Dillon, Doheny, O'Gorman, and McGee.—Arrest of O'Brien, Meagher, O'Donohoe, and McManus—Their trial and conviction—O'Brien's intrepidity—Character of O'Donohoe and McManus—Meagher's speech—Last of the Irish Confederation.

WHILE Duffy and the other prisoners were in confinement and the *Habeas Corpus* act was suspended, the Dublin Confederates could not make any demonstration whatever, even if their strength would have justified such a course. A few, indeed, left the city to join the leaders in the provinces; but the clubs, as it was always anticipated in case of an insurrection, were powerless. O'Brien, Dillon, Meagher, O'Donohoe, and McManus repaired to Tipperary whither Doheny had already gone. O'Gorman selected Limerick and Clare; and Reilly and Smith, the county of Kilkenny.

It is never pleasant to dwell on the failure of a national cause, particularly when, as was the case of the Confederates, its champions have proved individually brave, resolute, and thoroughly sincere. But the conduct of the people, from whom they hoped quite a different reception, must have quickly convinced them that all those qualities were useless, and that, so far from being able to arouse a warlike spirit among the peasantry by their appeals, they were generally looked upon with suspicion, if not dislike. What could eloquence and daring do with a crowd of half-starved and totally unarmed peasantry? Had they been of even higher hope and loftier attributes — leaders or generals who knew how to fight and control men in and out of action, which they certainly were not, they could neither have infused new life nor given successful direction to the mass of famished creatures, men, women, and children, who crowded around them, and who infinitely needed and preferred bread instead of bullets. The only incident which occurred previous to the arrest of O'Brien, proves this conclusively. On the morning of the 29th of

July, O'Brien and his friends being at Ballingarry, accompanied by a crowd of two or three hundred persons of both sexes, came in sight of a police force of forty-five men under Captain Grant. Grant, upon seeing who was in his front, instead of marching forward, turned off the road and took possession of Widow McCormack's house, a large stone building. O'Brien's followers surrounded the house; and upon Grant being ordered to surrender, he asked for half an hour to deliberate. This was granted; but before its expiration the people began to throw stones through the windows, some of which struck the commander and several of his men. The order was then given to fire: two of the peasantry were instantly killed, and several wounded. An attempt was made to fire the house, but failed; and a reënforcement of police coming in sight, the insurgents retreated in confusion. This was the last organized attempt at a rising; for, shortly after, the leaders separated, each to take care of himself as well as he could. Doheny, after innumerable wanderings, got to France by way of England; Dillon and Smith left Galway for America in August; O'Gorman took shipping from Cork for Constantinople; and McGee, after remaining in Derry and Donegal till all hope had vanished, left Lough Foyle for the United States, where he landed 10th October, 1848.

The fate of the others is soon told. On the 6th of August O'Brien was arrested at the railroad station in Thurles on his way home, having abandoned all hope of insurrection. Meagher and O'Donohoe were taken a week after on the road between Clonoulty and Hollycross; and on the seventh of September following, McManus was discovered and captured on board the ship *N. D. Chase*, in the Cove of Cork. The prisoners were sent to Kilmainham jail, where they were detained till a special commission was appointed at Clonmel. The trials commenced on the 28th of September, O'Brien being first put to the bar. Then followed that of McManus on the 9th of October; O'Donohoe's on the 13th, and Meagher's three days after.

These trials and their results were all of the same character—the same mockery of justice on the bench and corruption in the jury-box; but the government were resolved to secure convictions, and even the accused did not seem particularly anxious to palliate their "crimes," or avert the doom which they well knew had been predetermined in their case. Meanwhile, the public looked on half bewildered, if not wholly indifferent. They were all of course found guilty.

On the 9th of October the penalty of O'Brien's patriotism was pronounced. It read as follows:—

"That sentence is that you, William Smith O'Brien, be taken from hence to the place from whence you came, and be thence drawn on a hurdle to the place of execution, and be there hanged by the neck until you are dead; and that afterwards your head shall be severed from your body, and your body divided into four quarters, to be disposed of as her Majesty shall think fit. And may the Lord have mercy on your soul."

On the 23d of the same month the same sentence was pronounced on Meagher,

McManus, and O'Donohoe. The conduct of the condemned throughout was singularly firm and collected. "An eminent Queen's Counsel," said the *Freeman* of a subsequent date, "who was present during the awful ordeal, speaking of O'Brien, was heard to give utterance to a sentiment so truthfully graphic, that we record it in full: 'Well,' said he, his eyes full and his countenance flushed with emotion, 'never was there such a scene—never such true heroism displayed before. Emmet and Fitzgerald, and all combined, did not come up to that—so dignified, so calm, so heroic. He is a hero.'"—"My Lords," said O'Brien briefly, when asked the stereotyped question, "it is not my intention to enter into any vindication of my conduct, however much I have desired to avail myself of this opportunity of so doing. I am perfectly satisfied with the consciousness that I have performed my duty to my country—that I have done only that which, in my opinion, it was the duty of every Irishman to have done, and I am prepared to abide the consequences of having performed my duty to my native land. Proceed with your sentence."

Patrick O'Donohoe, always a man of few words, and, though a solicitor, one who would have handled a sword or musket better even than he did a pen, replied in a few brief words.

Terence Bellew McManus, who was next called up for judgment, was then about thirty years of age, of fine physique and a most genial and dauntless heart. He had been a playmate of Duffy, and left home with him for Dublin in quest of fortune. He afterwards removed to Liverpool, where by industry and intelligence he not only won a competency for himself, but was the chief promoter of every movement in that city for the advancement of his indigent countrymen. He was more of a worker than a speaker; and when he discovered that there was a prospect of fighting in Ireland, he promptly left his home and cast his lot with the Munster leaders. His address to the court was also short, but full of deep feeling and manliness. Meagher was next arraigned, and his speech was such as might have been expected from so noble and brilliant a victim. We are not aware that it has ever been fully and accurately reported, but the substance is doubtlessly contained in the following condensed sketch. He said:—

"My lords, it is my intention to say a few words only. I desire that the last act of a proceeding which has occupied so much of the public time should be of short duration. Nor have I the indelicate wish to close the dreary ceremony of a State Prosecution with a vain display of words. Did I fear that, hereafter, when I shall be no more, the country I have tried to serve would think ill of me, I might indeed avail myself of this solemn moment to vindicate my sentiments and my conduct. But I have no such fear. The country will judge of those sentiments and that conduct in a light far different from that in which the jury by whom I have been convicted have viewed them; and by the country the sentence which you, my lords, are about to pronounce, will be remembered only as the severe and solemn attestation of my rectitude and truth. Whatever be the language in which that sentence be spoken, I know that my fate will meet with sympathy, and that my memory will be honored. In speaking thus, accuse me not, my lords, of an indecorous presumption. To the efforts I have made in a just and noble cause I ascribe no vain importance—nor do I claim for those efforts any high reward. But it so happens, and it will ever happen so, that they who have tried to serve their country, no matter how weak the effort may have been, are sure to receive the thanks and the blessings of its people. With my country, then, I leave my memory—my sentiments —my acts—proudly feeling that they require no vindication from me this day. A jury of my countrymen, it is true, have found me guilty of the crime of which I stood indicted. For this I entertain not the slightest feeling of resentment toward them. Influenced as they must have been by the charge of the Lord Chief-Justice, they could have found no other verdict. What of that charge? Any strong observations on it, I feel sincerely, would ill befit the solemnity of this scene; but I would earnestly beseech of you, my lord,—you, who preside on that bench—when the passions and the prejudices of this hour have passed away, to appeal to your conscience, and ask if your charge was, as it ought to have been, impartial and indifferent between the subject and the crown. My lords, you may deem this language unbecoming in me, and, perhaps, it may seal my fate. But I am here to speak the truth, whatever it may cost. I am here to regret nothing I have ever done—to retract nothing I have ever said. I am here to crave, with no lying lip, the life I consecrate to the liberty of my country. Far from it: even here—here, where the thief, the libertine, the murderer, have left their footprints in the dust; here, on this spot, where the shadows of death surround me, and from which I see my early grave in an unanointed

soil opened to receive me,—even here, encircled by
these terrors, the hope which has beckoned me to the
perilous sea upon which I have been wrecked, still consoles, animates, enraptures me. No, I do not despair of
my poor old country, her peace, her liberty, her glory.
For that country I can do no more than bid her hope.
To lift this island up—to make her a benefactor to humanity, instead of being the meanest beggar in the
world—to restore to her her native powers and her ancient constitution,—this has been my ambition, and this
ambition has been my crime. Judged by the law of
England, I know this crime entails the penalty of
death; but the history of Ireland explains this crime,
and justifies it. Judged by that history, I am no
criminal—you (addressing Mr. McManus) are no
criminal—you (addressing Mr. Donohoe) are no
criminal—I deserve no punishment—we deserve no
punishment. Judged by that history, the treason of
which I stand convicted loses all its guilt, is sanctified
as a duty, will be ennobled as a sacrifice. With these
sentiments, my lord, I await the sentence of the court.
Having done what I felt to be my duty—having
spoken what I felt to be the truth, as I have done on
every other occasion of my short career, I now bid
farewell to the country of my birth, my passion, and
my death—the country whose misfortunes have invoked my sympathies—whose factions I have sought to
still—whose intellect I have prompted to a lofty aim—
whose freedom has been my fatal dream. I offer to
that country, as a proof of the love I bear her, and

of the sincerity with which I thought, and spoke, and struggled for her freedom—the life of a young heart, and with that life, all the hopes, the honors, the endearments of a happy and an honorable home. Pronounce, then, my lords, the sentence which the law directs, and I will be prepared to hear it. I trust I shall be prepared to meet its execution. I hope to be able, with a pure heart and perfect composure, to appear before a higher tribunal; a tribunal where a Judge of infinite goodness, as well as of justice, will preside, and where, my lords, many, many of the judgments of this world will be reversed."

A writ of error was sued out, on general grounds, but the judgment was confirmed by the Lords. Some of the people, without the knowledge or consent of the condemned, petitioned for a full pardon for them, but, as might have been expected, the prayer was denied. Their sentence, however, very much to their disappointment and chagrin, for they had no desire to live, was commuted to transportation for life, and on the 9th of July, 1849, they left Ireland in the ship of war *Swift* for Australia.

Thus closed the last act in the drama of '48. Looking back with the light of a quarter of a century's experience, it is very easy to point out the errors which were made and the mistakes committed by those highly gifted, enthusiastic, and thoroughly patriotic gentlemen; and had they possessed the gift of prophecy, which is seldom given to men for secular purposes, they might have seen and avoided in the future what many are but too ready to condemn in the retrospect. While we are willing to admit that there was not among them a man who had the least practical experience of military affairs, nor many who were used to the science of government, we cannot deny them those qualities which, if not conducive to success, bring no disgrace to defeat,—genius, eloquence, a keen sense of honor, and varied literary attainments,—gifts which would have been prized and admired in a free government, but which unfortunately are of little account in an armed revolution. It were idle now to speculate on what might have been the result if the Irish Confederation, uninfluenced by the French revolution of 1848, had pursued the even tenor of its way, organizing the country into clubs and keeping clear of the meshes of the law, till in a position to defy it, if necessary. The die was cast, the movement that promised so fair of success failed, and it will be for the men of this or another generation, who may take up the struggle, to profit by the mistakes of their predecessors.

CHAPTER XIV.

The literature of the Young Ireland party—James Clarence Mangan—Denis Florence McCarthy—Richard D'Alton Williams—Lady Wilde—The Library of Ireland—Davis, Duffy, Father Meehan, Doheny, McNevin, Mitchel, McGee, McCarthy, and Mrs. Callan—Their legacy to Young Ireland of to-day.

As an offset to the failure of their political projects, the "Young Irelanders," the "Irish Confederates," or the "Men of '48," as they have been indifferently called, left, not only bright examples of their steadfastness of purpose and unswerving hostility to all English parties inimical to Ireland, but they have bequeathed to Ireland the germs of a national literature which, under more favorable auspices, will, it is to be hoped, grow up and fructify in that land of poesy and eloquence. The five volumes of the *Nation* would of themselves, if nothing else of the writings of its contributors remained, form a small library of prose and poetry, more valuable than scores of ordinary books. The massive prose of Duffy, the electric poetry of Davis, the sharp, intense leaders of Mitchel, the solid, practical reports of McGee, the erudite reviews of Reilly, the lighter, but exceedingly pleasant sketches of Meagher, and the songs and ballads of most of those, and of scores of volunteer contributors, form a cyclopædia of politics, literature, and verse, unmatched in the history of journalism.

But those men, so full of national ideas, did not limit themselves to the columns of a newspaper. They established and carried on for nearly two years a series of monthly publications known as the "Library of Ireland," issued by Mr. James Duffy of Dublin, and at the same time contributed valuable articles to that publisher's *Catholic Magazine*, the *University Magazine*, and other periodicals and journals, besides separate volumes published by various houses in the metropolis.

Thus James Clarence Mangan, one of the earliest poetical contributors to the *Nation*, as well as the most original, often enlivened the pages of the *University* by his quaint, but deeply impassioned odes and songs, some of which were translated from the Irish, and others from the German. The latter, collected in two handsome volumes in 1847, were most favorably received by the public and press. Mangan was a native of Meath and died in 1849, when scarcely middle-aged, leaving a large number of fugitive pieces, many of which were afterwards published in book form by Mr. Ellis.

Denis Florence McCarthy, also another of the *Nation's* volunteer staff, still we are happy to say in the land of the living, has generally been looked upon as the sweetest and most accomplished poet the country has produced since the days of Moore, and even in some particulars he has been regarded, not without reason, as superior to Ireland's immortal bard. His detached Irish ballads and songs have been published from time to time in separate volumes, and his translations of Camoens, Lope de Vega, and other Portuguese and Spanish writers, have won high approbation not only in Europe, but among our best critics in this country.

Richard D'Alton Williams, whose name has been already mentioned in connection with the *Irish Tribune*, first attracted attention by the appearance in the *Nation* of his "Misadventures of a Medical Student," a series of poetical sketches, irresistibly comic and full of genuine humor. But his genius took a higher flight as he advanced in years, and some of the most powerful as well as the most pathetic songs written in the *Nation* during the Repeal agitation and the famine, were from the pen of "Shamrock," his usual *nom-de-plume*. We are not aware that his contributions to the literature of the period has yet been collected in a permanent form. He emigrated to this country in 1850, and died in the South during the late war, while pursuing his calling as a physician.

There were others, also, who added their tributary streams of song to the general flood of poesy which overflowed the land from 1843 till the failure of '48; men of much merit, and great sweetness and healthfulness of tone. They were Thomas Davis, "the Belfast man;" (I. De Jean) Frazer, from the Brosna's banks; Michael J. Barry, of Cork; "The Kilkenny man;" Pigot, son of the Chief Baron of that name; McDermott, of Paris; Samuel Ferguson, and a host of others of lesser light, or whose mask has been so impenetrable that, though their verse is admired, their names are altogether unknown.

There were female poets, also,—women with large hearts, warm sympathies, and passionate attachment to their native land, who could wield a pen and weave a song as deftly as they could ply the needle or adorn the embroidery frame. Preëminent among those was "Speranza," a woman of remarkable depth of mind and power of expression. Some of the best prose articles which appeared in the *Nation* in 1847-8, were written by her, but she is best known for her poetry, which was ever powerful, elevating, full of rhythm, and sparkling with original ideas. Besides her, like sister graces, were "Mary" and "Eva," who, if less masculine in genius, were her compeers in melody and beauty.

The Library of Ireland, of which there appeared twenty-two monthly volumes, was, with few exceptions, devoted to historical works and essays relating to Ireland, written by the Young Ireland party. The exceptions were, "The Ballad Poetry of Ireland," edited by Duffy; and "Davis Poems" by Wallis, and one or two works of fiction written by William Carleton. The most prominent and the most instructive of those books may be classed as follows:—

In History: "The History of the Geraldines," translated from Dominicus O'Daly, by the Rev. C. P. Meehan, who has since become so well known as the translator of "Lanzi History of Painting;" "The Franciscan in Ireland," and other works; "The Confederation of Kilkenny," an original work on Irish history from 1640 to 1652, by the same author, and the "Writings of Bishop French," which, if we are not mistaken, were edited by the same learned clergyman.

"The American Revolution," by Michael Doheny, is a succinct and readable account of our own struggle for independence, and was particularly useful at that time in Ireland, where nearly all the school books and histories used were written from an English stand-point, and, of course, were full of prejudice and misstatement.

"The Confiscation of Ulster" and "The Volunteers of '82," written by Thomas McNevin, are also reliable and carefully written books.

In Biography: John Mitchel's "Life of Hugh O'Neil" deservedly holds a very prominent place. It is a clear, animated, brilliant, and withal truthful account of the career of one of the greatest soldiers and most astute statesmen that modern Ireland has produced. The man who actually defied the whole power of Elizabeth for so many years, and who might, if any one could, have united Ireland and freed her at the same time, deserved a good biographer and found one.

"The life of Art. McMorrough," and "The

Irish Writers," by Thomas D'Arcy McGee, are historical as well as biographical sketches of two very different epochs, the thirteenth century, the first succeeding the invasion; and the seventeenth, when the scholars of Ireland, driven from home by the penal laws, were to be found in every part of the continent. On the appearance of the latter work, the *Dublin Mail* remarked: "It is a record of the historians and churchmen of that troubled period, written in a masculine and philosophic style, and in a tone of impartiality most excellent."

"The Poets and Dramatists of Ireland," of which Denis Florence McCarthy was the author, is a most readable work, and none the less attractive that it was written by a brother poet. "It is," said the *Cork Examiner*, "a collection of concise, but comprehensive biographies, presented along with an elegant introduction. Many of those considered to belong solely to the sister country, are here re-claimed for this, and thus further commended to our partialities. The epitomized lives are given with judgment, and nothing essential is forgotten in the personal or intellectual delineation of character."

Essays : "The Casket of Irish Pearls," a number of essays on Irish subjects selected from the best authors, was collected by Mrs. Callan under the name of "Thornton McMahon."

"Davis Essays," edited by Duffy, are too well known and too highly appreciated to need comment. A new and much improved edition of them was lately brought out in this country.

All those works were exceedingly popular at the time of their first appearance, and many of them have run into numerous editions and still keep their place in the fore-rank of Irish literature. They were all written or edited by men of superior knowledge, of a high order of ability, and for a purpose,—that purpose being the elevation and purification of the public taste, the instruction of the masses, and the infusion of correct ideas and sound national sentiment into the minds of the youth of Ireland.

Thus we see that the men of '48,—some of whom have long since passed away, and others are yet among us who have not, we are happy to say, outlived their earlier affections,—have left us some "footprints on the sands of time" which cannot be erased, and which the young Irishmen of to-day may follow with advantage. Let us hope, too, that, while those of the present generation criticise with moderation the political defects of the men who deserved freedom, even if they did not achieve it, they will not forget those literary memorials of their genius, so that they also may help "to create and to foster a public opinion in Ireland, and to make it racy of the soil."

THE END.

www.ingramcontent.com/pod-product-compliance
Lightning Source LLC
Chambersburg PA
CBHW022025240426
43667CB00042B/1194